FlashKids SUMMER

2nd Grade

Jumpstart second grade with fun skill-building activities!

FlashKids

New York

New York

An Imprint of Sterling Publishing Co., Inc.

FLASH KIDS and the distinctive Flash Kids logo are registered trademarks
of Barnes and Noble, Inc.

Text © 2016 by Sterling Publishing Co., Inc.

ISBN 978-1-4114-8065-0

Distributed in Canada by Sterling Publishing Co., Inc.
℅ Canadian Manda Group, 664 Annette Street
Toronto, Ontario, M6S 2C8, Canada
Distributed in the United Kingdom by GMC Distribution Services
Castle Place, 166 High Street, Lewes, East Sussex, BN7 1XU, England
Distributed in Australia by NewSouth Books
University of New South Wales, Sydney, NSW 2052, Australia

For information about custom editions, special sales, and premium
and corporate purchases, please contact Sterling Special Sales
at specialsales@sterlingpublishing.com.

Manufactured in Malaysia
Lot #:
2 4 6 8 10 9 7 5 3 1
11/21

sterlingpublishing.com

Cover illustration: Justin Poulter

Front cover image: shapecharge/iStock/Getty Images Plus
Back cover image: IndigoLT/iStock/Getty Images Plus
All interior images by Dreamstime, iStockphoto, Shutterstock,
Thinkstock, and Wikimedia Foundation with the following exceptions:
© Dorling Kindersley/Getty Images (map); © Chad Ehlers/Alamy (pool party).

Dear Caregiver,

As a caregiver, you want your child to have time to relax and have fun during the summer, but you don't want your child's math and reading skills to get rusty. How do you make time for summer fun while ensuring that your child will be ready for the next school year?

The *Flash Kids Summer* workbook provides short, fun activities to help children keep their skills fresh all summer long. This book not only reviews what students learned during first grade, it also introduces what they'll be learning in second grade. Best of all, the games, puzzles, and stories help students retain their knowledge as well as build new skills. By the time your child finishes the book, they will be ready for a smooth transition into the next school year.

As your child completes the activities in this book, shower them with encouragement and praise. You can feel good knowing that you are taking an active and important role in your child's education. Helping your child complete the activities in this book is providing an excellent example— that you value learning every day! Have a wonderful summer, and most of all have fun learning together!

Joke Time

Complete the activity below.

Write the numbers that come before and after.

$\underset{A}{\underline{3}}$ **4** $\underset{L}{\underline{5}}$ $\underset{B}{\underline{}}$ **9** $\underset{T}{\underline{}}$ $\underset{E}{\underline{}}$ **19** $\underset{O}{\underline{}}$

$\underset{T}{\underline{}}$ **12** $\underset{P}{\underline{}}$ $\underset{Y}{\underline{}}$ **7** $\underset{I}{\underline{}}$ $\underset{W}{\underline{}}$ **15** $\underset{C}{\underline{}}$

Unscramble each set of numbers and write them in order from smallest to biggest.

16   13   14   12   15 $\underset{H}{\underline{12}}$ $\underset{K}{\underline{}}$ $\underset{R}{\underline{}}$ $\underset{E}{\underline{}}$ $\underset{S}{\underline{}}$

22   25   21   23   24 $\underset{D}{\underline{}}$ $\underset{C}{\underline{}}$ $\underset{O}{\underline{}}$ $\underset{G}{\underline{}}$ $\underset{U}{\underline{}}$

Now unscramble and write the numbers from biggest to smallest.

7   4   5   8   6 $\underset{J}{\underline{8}}$ $\underset{N}{\underline{}}$ $\underset{S}{\underline{}}$ $\underset{A}{\underline{}}$ $\underset{T}{\underline{}}$

18   16   20   17   19 $\underset{M}{\underline{}}$ $\underset{E}{\underline{}}$ $\underset{V}{\underline{}}$ $\underset{R}{\underline{}}$ $\underset{X}{\underline{}}$

Find each number above and write the letter to complete the joke.

Where do numbers like to eat lunch?

$\underset{3}{\underline{A}}$ $\underset{10}{\underline{}}$ $\underset{11}{\underline{}}$ $\underset{12}{\underline{}}$ $\underset{15}{\underline{}}$

$\underset{22}{\underline{}}$ $\underset{23}{\underline{}}$ $\underset{25}{\underline{}}$ $\underset{7}{\underline{}}$ $\underset{4}{\underline{}}$ $\underset{19}{\underline{}}$ $\underset{17}{\underline{}}$

The First Ferris Wheel

Read the story. Then answer the questions.

George W. Ferris was a man with big ideas. In 1893, a big fair was being planned in Chicago. George built a ride that looked like a giant wheel. It was 250 feet wide and had 36 cars. Each car could hold 60 people. They called it the Ferris wheel.

1. What is this passage about?
   a) the first Ferris wheel
   b) the first fair

2. How wide was the Ferris wheel?
   a) 250 feet
   b) 60 feet

3. Who was George W. Ferris?
   a) The first man to go to the fair
   b) The man who built the first Ferris wheel

4. Why was the ride called a Ferris wheel?
   a) Because it had 36 cars
   b) Because George Ferris built it

Hiking Trails

The numbers on each path follow a pattern. Write numbers on the lines to complete each path. Then write the pattern. The first one is done for you.

1. **2**   **4**   _6_   **8**   **10**   _12_   _14_   **16**   _18_   **20**

    Pattern: _+2_

2. **2**   ___   **4**   **5**   **6**   ___   ___   **9**   **10**   ___   **12**

    Pattern: _____

3. **3**   **6**   ___   **12**   **15**   ___   **21**   ___   **27**   ___

    Pattern: _____

4. **5**   ___   **15**   **20**   ___   **30**   **35**   ___   **45**

    Pattern: _____

Pretty Patterns

Repeat the patterns.

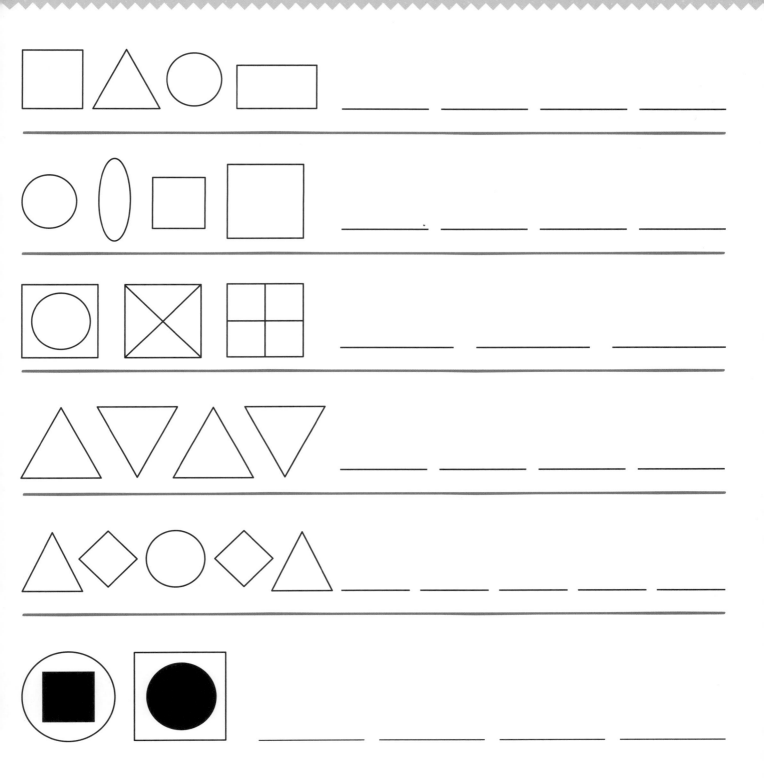

Word Search

Find the words and circle them. Words can go across or down.

again	know	live	any	when
put	after	every	could	then

```
o   a   g   a   i   n   o   o   o
o   f   a   n   l   y   c   u
e   t   n   y   t   p   u   t
v   e   k   w   h   a   t   h
e   r   n   l   i   v   e   e
r   c   o   u   l   d   v   n
y   o   w   h   e   n   r   y
```

Building Words

Below are the mixed-up letters of a word. How many little words can you make from the letters? Can you find the big word?

o r h m e t

1. Words with 2 letters:

_____

_____

_____

2. Words with 3 letters:

_____

_____

_____

_____

_____

3. Words with 4 letters:

_____

_____

_____

4. Word with 5 letters:

_____

5. Word with 6 letters (the big word):

_____

Amazing Adjectives

An adjective describes a person, place, or thing.
Circle the adjectives in each sentence.

1. Lisa's (white) puppy played in the (muddy) puddle.

2. The tiny mouse ate bits of yellow cheese.

3. The large zoo was full of noisy animals.

4. Her short hair was curly and soft.

5. Mia took a long nap under the shady tree.

6. The crisp apple tasted sweet.

7. My new teacher gave us tasty cupcakes.

8. Tennis is a fun game to play on a warm day.

9. My brother is smart and funny.

10. Jess ate a slice of spicy, hot pizza.

Add and Circle

Add. Then circle the number that is bigger in each box.

1.

$$\begin{array}{r} 4 \\ + 3 \\ \hline \end{array} \qquad \begin{array}{r} 5 \\ + 1 \\ \hline \end{array}$$

2.

$$\begin{array}{r} 2 \\ + 6 \\ \hline \end{array} \qquad \begin{array}{r} 4 \\ + 0 \\ \hline \end{array}$$

3.

$$\begin{array}{r} 1 \\ + 7 \\ \hline \end{array} \qquad \begin{array}{r} 3 \\ + 3 \\ \hline \end{array}$$

4.

$$\begin{array}{r} 0 \\ + 5 \\ \hline \end{array} \qquad \begin{array}{r} 2 \\ + 2 \\ \hline \end{array}$$

5.

$$\begin{array}{r} 4 \\ + 1 \\ \hline \end{array} \qquad \begin{array}{r} 2 \\ + 8 \\ \hline \end{array}$$

6.

$$\begin{array}{r} 1 \\ + 6 \\ \hline \end{array} \qquad \begin{array}{r} 8 \\ + 1 \\ \hline \end{array}$$

7.

$$\begin{array}{r} 5 \\ + 4 \\ \hline \end{array} \qquad \begin{array}{r} 5 \\ + 5 \\ \hline \end{array}$$

8.

$$\begin{array}{r} 0 \\ + 9 \\ \hline \end{array} \qquad \begin{array}{r} 3 \\ + 7 \\ \hline \end{array}$$

A Friend to the End

Complete the activity below.

A **telling** sentence ends with a period:

I have no lunch.

An **asking** sentence ends with a question mark.

Do you want some?

End each sentence with a period or a question mark.

1. Where is your lunch _____

2. I left my lunch at home _____

3. I can share my lunch _____

4. Do you like apples _____

5. Can I have a bite _____

6. You are a good friend _____

In the Beginning

Write the beginning letters **ch** or **sh** to complete each word.

_ch_ air

_____ eep

_____ oe

_____ ell

_____ eese

_____ icken

_____ ild

_____ ip

Healthful Habits

Some activities will keep you healthy. Circle the pictures that show children doing healthy activities.

Maze Cafe

Count by 5s to find your way through the maze. Follow the trail and see what's for lunch at the cafe.

CAFE

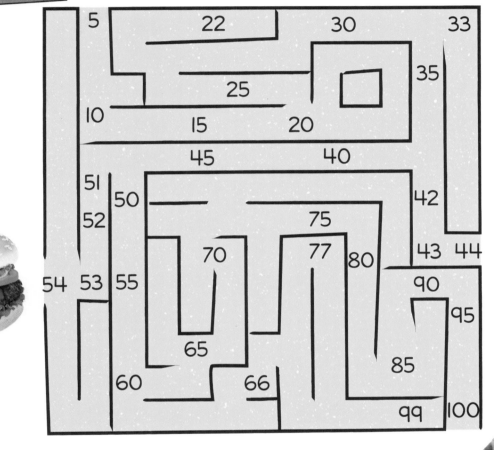

Count by 5s.

5	10			25			40	
		65			80			100

Show and Tell

Complete the activity below.

Complete the telling sentences about the picture. Then write two of your own.

1. This is my pet bird ☐

2. The bird _____

_____

3. _____

What would you ask the boy about his bird?
Complete the asking sentences. Then write two of your own.

4. What does the bird eat ☐

5. How _____

6. _____

_____

Find the Number Words

Find and circle the number words for **1** to **12** in the word search.
Words can go across or down.

one	two	three	four	five	six
seven	eight	nine	ten	eleven	twelve

A	B	H	Y	J	K	M	L	T	D
O	N	E	J	N	T	F	C	W	N
Y	V	F	S	P	Q	S	X	E	A
G	E	I	G	H	T	I	U	L	S
W	S	V	B	Y	C	X	X	V	E
H	B	E	T	H	R	E	E	E	V
T	E	N	M	Y	T	Z	S	T	E
H	B	G	F	O	U	R	G	W	N
M	N	N	I	N	E	M	E	O	A
E	L	E	V	E	N	H	N	Y	B

Space Race

Subtract. Find the answer on the space race and cross it out.
See which rocket gets to the moon first!

9   10

1   7

5   8

3   6

~~4~~   2

A   B

1.
$$\begin{array}{r} 8 \\ -\ 4 \\ \hline 4 \end{array}$$

2.
$$\begin{array}{r} 5 \\ -\ 2 \\ \hline \end{array}$$

3.
$$\begin{array}{r} 4 \\ -\ 2 \\ \hline \end{array}$$

4.
$$\begin{array}{r} 9 \\ -\ 3 \\ \hline \end{array}$$

5.
$$\begin{array}{r} 9 \\ -\ 1 \\ \hline \end{array}$$

6.
$$\begin{array}{r} 10 \\ -\ 5 \\ \hline \end{array}$$

7.
$$\begin{array}{r} 6 \\ -\ 5 \\ \hline \end{array}$$

8.
$$\begin{array}{r} 9 \\ -\ 2 \\ \hline \end{array}$$

9.
$$\begin{array}{r} 9 \\ -\ 0 \\ \hline \end{array}$$

10.
$$\begin{array}{r} 12 \\ -\ 2 \\ \hline \end{array}$$

Lots of Letters

Write the beginning and the ending letters.

1.

__s__ i __x__

2.

___ u ___

3.

___ a ___

4.

___ o ___

5.

___ e ___

6.

___ i ___

7.

___ i ___

8.

___ u ___

9.

___ a ___

If the two pictures have the same beginning sound, circle **beginning**.
If they have the same ending sound, circle **ending**.

10.

Beginning
Ending

11.

Beginning
Ending

12.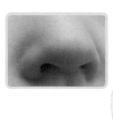

Beginning
Ending

Subtraction Action

There are 10 subtraction problems in this puzzle.
Each problem can go down or across. Circle each problem.

Here is an example.

11	5	7
6	4	2
10	1	8

12	15	13	5	11
6	10	8	2	6
6	3	5	4	5
3	7	2	5	12
3	0	3	10	7

Making Halves

When you divide something in half, you divide it into two equal parts.
Circle one-half of each group of objects.

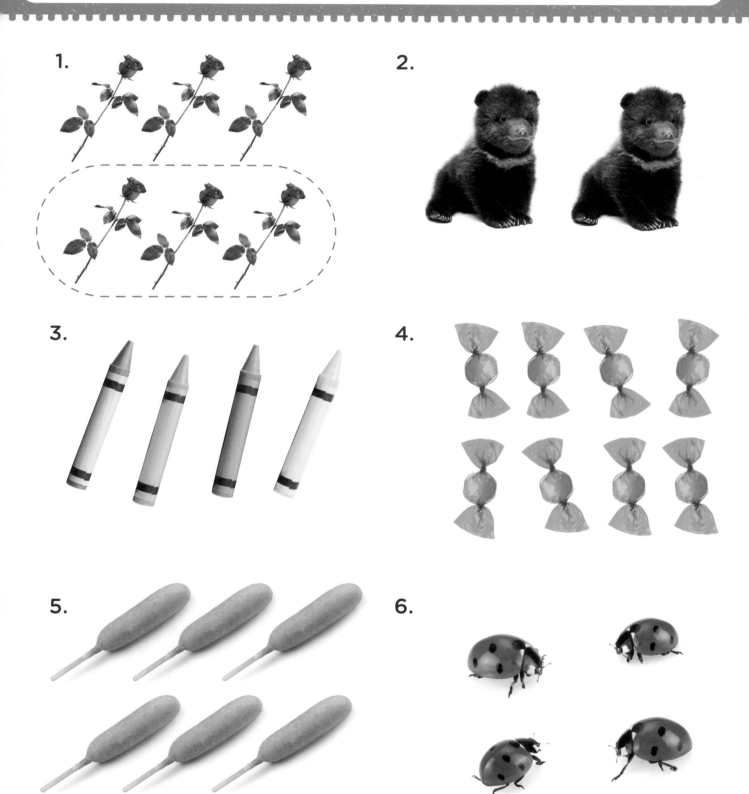

1.

2.

3.

4.

5.

6.

Clowning Around

Write the missing numbers from 51 to 100.

		T		R			T	A	
51	52	__	54	__	56	57	__	__	60
U			B		L			N	
__	62	63	64	__	66	__	68	69	__
	O	S			E			N	
71	__	__	74	75	__	77	78	__	80
D			F			P			D
__	82	83	__	85	86	__	88	89	__
	O			V	E		E		
91	__	93	94	__	__	97	__	99	100

Find each number above and
write the letter to complete the joke.

How high did the silly clown count?

__ __   __ __ __
53 92   72 70 98

__ __ __ __ __ __ __
84 61 79 81 55 96 90

Mini Golf

Number the sentences to show the order of events in the story.

_____ The course started with some easy holes.

_____ Sofia and her friends went to the mini golf course.

_____ The hole was on a narrow bridge above the water.

_____ They rented clubs and balls and started the game.

_____ Andy's ball rolled off the bridge and splashed into the water.

_____ Then they got to a very tricky hole surrounded by water.

Connect each word with its meaning.

1. course   a) to pay money to use something

2. rented   b) not very wide

3. tricky   c) a series of challenges

4. narrow   d) difficult

Action Words

A **verb** is an action word. It tells what a person or object is doing.
Circle the verbs in this paragraph.

Last week I got a puppy. He has floppy ears and big brown eyes. He barks at the cat. He also chases butterflies and bees in the backyard. We walk to the park on Saturdays and play together. He is very friendly. Everyone loves him! I showed him how to jump in the air and catch balls. We go everywhere together. He is a good friend, so I named him Buddy. He comes whenever I call him by his name!

1. How many verbs are there? _____

Now, fill in the blanks with your own action words.

2. The lizard _____ up the wall.

3. My cat _____ in the sun.

4. The red car _____ down the street.

5. A snake _____ in the jungle.

6. I love to _____ in the sun.

Nifty Nouns

A **noun** is a person, place, or thing. Circle the noun in each row.

1. under   jump   (sock)   happy

2. kitten   sing   walk   pink

3. hear   swim   tiny   apple

4. loud   baby   blue   fluffy

5. child   fun   windy   sleep

6. drive   cold   beach   stop

7. silly   eat   milk   talk

8. dinosaur   over   pretty   skip

9. brown   sour   tasty   zoo

10. tall   open   home   ran

Coin Count

Circle the coin or the coins that equal the value on the left.

1¢

5¢

10¢

25¢

10¢

15¢

Happy Endings

Complete each sentence with the singular or the plural word.
Use the picture clues and the word box to help.

ribbon	tree	sock	wheel
fox	bike	tire	rock

1. I found my lucky racing _____.

2. It was time for the _____ race!

3. I raced along a path lined with _____ in the sun.

4. I saw two _____ playing in the woods.

5. There were sharp _____ on the ground.

6. I thought I had a flat _____.

7. It was just a rock stuck in my _____.

8. I finished the race and got a _____.

Picture Rhymes

Finish writing the name of each picture.
Then draw a line between each pair of rhyming words.

1. c _____

2. m _____

3. b _____

4. b _____

5. h _____

6. b _____

7. g _____

8. t _____

Parts of a Plant

Do you know all the parts of a plant?
Label each part using the words in the box.

stem

flower

seedling

leaf

roots

flower

Parts of a Plant

Flip Out!

Add. Then flip the numbers in each question and add again.

You can swap the numbers you're adding and get the same answer!

$$3 + 4 = 7 \longrightarrow 4 + 3 = 7$$

1. $2 + 3 = \underline{5}$

   $\underline{3} + \underline{2} = \underline{5}$

2. $6 + 4 = \underline{}$

   $\underline{} + \underline{} = \underline{}$

3. $5 + 2 = \underline{}$

   $\underline{} + \underline{} = \underline{}$

4. $2 + 9 = \underline{}$

   $\underline{} + \underline{} = \underline{}$

5. $6 + 3 = \underline{}$

   $\underline{} + \underline{} = \underline{}$

6. $9 + 1 = \underline{}$

   $\underline{} + \underline{} = \underline{}$

7. $7 + 5 = \underline{}$

   $\underline{} + \underline{} = \underline{}$

8. $3 + 8 = \underline{}$

   $\underline{} + \underline{} = \underline{}$

Sunny Sentences

Complete the activity below.

Use capitals for:

- First word of a sentence
- The word "I"
- Places
- People's names

This summer **I** went to **H**awaii with **A**my.

Rewrite each sentence with correct capitilization.

1. We got on the plane in los angeles.

   We got on the plane in Los Angeles.

2. our plane landed in honolulu.

   _____

3. then amy and I flew to maui.

   _____

4. amy's sister peg lives in maui.

   _____

5. peg took amy and me swimming.

   _____

6. i want to go to hawaii again!

   _____

Where Does It Come From?

Everything we eat, use, or wear comes from somewhere. Some things are made and then sold in markets. Some things come from plants and animals.

Draw a line matching each object to the place it came from.

Finish the Pattern

Look at each row of numbers. Can you see a pattern? Finish each pattern.
Then write the pattern.

1. 2   5   8   11   _14_   _17_   _20_

Pattern: _+3_

2. 1   5   9   13   _____   _____   _____

Pattern: _____

3. 14   12   _____   8   _____   _____   2

Pattern: _____

4. 3   6   9   _____   15   _____   _____

Pattern: _____

5. 10   9   8   _____   _____   _____   4   _____

Pattern: _____

6. 10   15   20   _____   30   _____   _____

Pattern: _____

Pool Party

Complete the activity below.

List things you see in and around the pool:

_____ _____ _____ _____

_____ _____ _____ _____

_____ _____ _____ _____

Describe the kids. What are they doing and wearing?

_____

_____

_____

_____

What kind of day is it?

_____

_____

Early or Late?

Look at the time on each clock.
Then circle **early** or **late** to finish each sentence.

1.

School starts at 8:00.
Jesse is (early) late.

2.

Soccer practice is at 3:45.
Mia is **early late**.

3.

The dog is walked at 10:30.
McKenzie is **early late**.

4.

Dinner is at 6:00.
Devon is **early late**.

5.

Dance class begins at noon.
Keisha is **early late**.

6.

The picnic is at 2:15.
Noah is **early late**.

Weigh It!

Look at each picture. Which unit of measure would you use?
Circle **ounces** or **pounds**.

(ounces)   pounds

ounces   pounds

ounces   pounds

ounces   pounds

ounces   pounds

ounces   pounds

ounces   pounds

ounces   pounds

Track Times

Write the time below each clock. Find the time on the track and cross it out.
See which runner goes all the way!

Runner A: ~~10:00~~ — 2:30 — 4:30 — 11:00 — 12:30

Runner B: 6:00 — 8:00 — 5:30 — 7:00 — 6:30

1.

10:00

2.

_____

3.

_____

4.

_____

5.

_____

6.

_____

7.

_____

8.

_____

9.

_____

The Long and Short of It

Add **e** to make the long vowel sound.

1.

cap   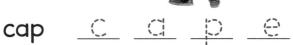 c a p e

2.

tub __ __ __ __

3.

can __ __ __ __

4.

tap __ __ __ __

Add or take away the **e** to change the vowel sound.

5. __ __ __ hide

6. hop __ __ __ __

7. fin __ __ __ __

8. __ __ __ bite

9. __ __ __ note

10. mop __ __ __ __

11. __ __ __ made

12. rod __ __ __ __

At the End

Look at each picture. Say its name aloud. Then circle the word in each row with the same ending sound.

1. tub   stop   (match)   lock

2. star   bath   beach   bell

3. wash   catch   boot   glass

4. laugh   tax   pink   radish

5. rug   pack   cent   jar

6. sky   finish   cart   hear

Windy Words

Write the best word to complete each sentence.
Use words from the word box.

branch	school	day	lights	spooky
dinner	bed	story	papers	hair
	fell	friend	shook	

Today was a very windy __day__ ! On my way to

_____, my hat blew down the street. My _____

was a mess! At school, I dropped my notebook and _____

went flying everywhere. My best _____ Joshua helped me catch

them. When I got home, a _____ had blown off our tree.

It _____ in the yard. When the _____ went out,

we had to use candles to see. It was fun to eat _____ with

candles. Later, Dad told us a scary _____. Then, when I

was in _____, the wind _____ the windows.

It was _____!

Now, draw a picture of a windy day.

Add-venture Time!

Add the three numbers and write the answer.

1.
$$\begin{array}{r} 2 \\ 4 \\ +\ 1 \\ \hline \textbf{H} \end{array}$$

2.
$$\begin{array}{r} 5 \\ 2 \\ +\ 2 \\ \hline \textbf{E} \end{array}$$

3.
$$\begin{array}{r} 2 \\ 3 \\ +\ 3 \\ \hline \textbf{N} \end{array}$$

4.
$$\begin{array}{r} 4 \\ 2 \\ +\ 4 \\ \hline \textbf{I} \end{array}$$

5.
$$\begin{array}{r} 8 \\ 3 \\ +\ 3 \\ \hline \textbf{G} \end{array}$$

6.
$$\begin{array}{r} 6 \\ 3 \\ +\ 2 \\ \hline \textbf{C} \end{array}$$

7.
$$\begin{array}{r} 9 \\ 3 \\ +\ 1 \\ \hline \textbf{E} \end{array}$$

8.
$$\begin{array}{r} 3 \\ 4 \\ +\ 5 \\ \hline \textbf{!} \end{array}$$

9.
$$\begin{array}{r} 7 \\ 5 \\ +\ 3 \\ \hline \textbf{T} \end{array}$$

Find each number in the answers above and write the matching letter to complete the joke.

What was T. Rex's favorite number?

E ___ ___ ___ ___ ___
9   10   14   7   15   12

Larry and Gary

Read the story. Then complete the activity.

Larry and Gary wanted to do something special for their mother's birthday. Their mother loved flowers. Larry was artistic, so he painted a picture of a flower garden. Gary had good business ideas, so he started a lemonade stand. With the money he earned, he bought his mother some flowers. Both boys had worked hard to give their mother nice gifts. She had a very happy birthday.

Check whether the statement describes Larry, Gary, or both boys.

	Larry	Gary	Both
1. Wanted to do something special			✓
2. Was very artistic			
3. Earned money to buy flowers			
4. Worked hard to give a nice present			
5. Painted a picture of a flower garden			
6. Had good business ideas			

Two Words in One

A compound word is a word formed by combining two words. To make compound words below, write the word for each picture. Then draw a line from the word to another word on the right. These two words will make a compound word!

1. _____bird_____   ball

2. _____   fish

3. _____   bow

4. _____   house

5. _____   bell

6. _____   shine

7. _____   cake

8. _____   place

Write the compound words below.

1. _____birdhouse_____   2. _____

3. _____   4. _____

5. _____   6. _____

7. _____   8. _____

Solid, Liquid, Gas

Matter comes in three different states. The states are **solid**, **liquid**, and **gas**. Water can be all three states: ice, water, and steam. Label each picture below as a **solid**, **liquid**, or **gas**.

ice

water

steam

_____   _____   _____

Write **solid**, **liquid**, or **gas** after each word to tell what it is.

1. milk ___liquid___

2. rock _____

3. air _____

4. clay _____

5. honey _____

6. oil _____

7. steam _____

8. baseball _____

9. book _____

10. juice _____

Do You Measure Up?

Complete the activity below.

Use the ruler to measure each line, and write it below.

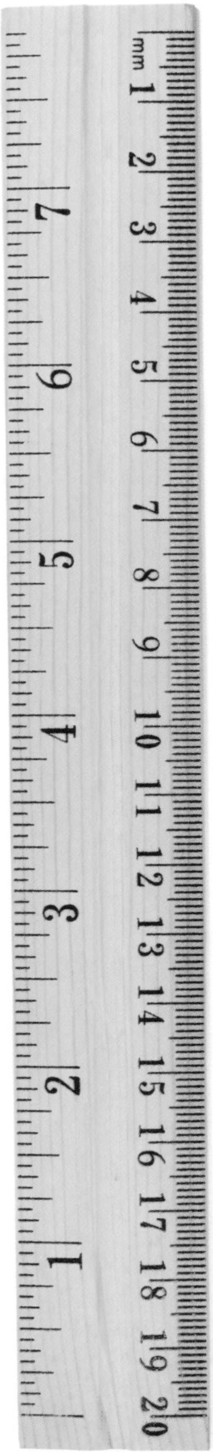

Use the ruler to draw lines that equal the numbers below.

3
___
inches

___
inches

___
inches

3
inches

6
inches

4
inches

Wacky Words

Draw a line to connect the word parts.

rain	room
bed	fly
snow	ball
butter	bow
side	man
foot	walk

Write the word that goes with the picture clues. Use the words from above.

1.

_____

2.

_____

3.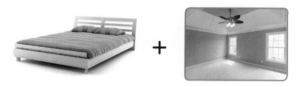

_____

4.

_____

5.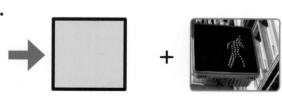

_____

6.

_____

What Doesn't Belong?

Look at each row of objects. Cross out the object in each group that doesn't belong. Then circle the objects that belong.

1.

2.

3.

4.

Math Munchies

Add or subtract to solve the problems.

1. Andy has 3 apples, and Sue has 2. How many apples do they have altogether?

_____ apples

2. Steve had 8 cookies. He gave 4 to Brian. How many cookies does Steve have now?

_____ cookies

3. Alex has 5 mushrooms and 6 peppers on his pizza slice. How many toppings does he have altogether?

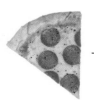

_____ toppings

4. Sara had 15 french fries, and she gave 5 to Jason. How many fries does Sara have left?

_____ fries

5. Jane has 6 blueberries. Her dad gave her 6 strawberries. How many berries does she have altogether?

_____ berries

6. Bob had 12 peanuts in the bag. He dropped 4 on the ground. How many peanuts are left?

_____ peanuts

Name That Noun

Complete the activity below.

A **noun** is a person, a place, or a thing.

Tom reads **books** at **school**.

Circle the words that are nouns.

write   boy   cap   sit

smart   pencil   paper   read

Now write some nouns you see in the picture:

_____   _____   _____

Circle the noun in each sentence.

1. Sit quietly at your desk.

2. Open your book, please.

3. Take out a pen.

4. Use some paper for writing.

Sunny Words

Many things are organized in **alphabetical order**. This means they are arranged in order from **A** to **Z**, like words in a dictionary.
Rewrite each set of words in alphabetical order.

tiger
baboon
giraffe
lion

chair
dresser
bed
table

lunch
dinner
breakfast
snack

desk
pencil
book
student

1. baboon
   giraffe
   lion
   tiger

2. _____

3. _____

4. _____

summer
winter
fall
autumn

beach
park
zoo
mall

starfish
crab
whale
lobster

puppy
kitten
goldfish
mouse

5. _____

6. _____

7. _____

8. _____

Write It Right

Rewrite each sentence correctly.
Use the correct capitalization and punctuation.

1. my family went to the beach last saturday

   My family went to the beach last Saturday.

2. it was a warm and breezy Summer Day

   _____

3. my Brother carlos swam in the Ocean

   _____

4. i played in the sand and built a big Sand castle

   _____

5. carlos and i hunted for shells along the seashore

   _____

6. we found pink white, and purple shells

   _____

7. My dad made a big bonfire to cook Dinner

   _____

8. we ate hot dogs chips and crispy vegetables

   _____

9. the Ocean smelled fresh and salty

   _____

10. do you think we can come back next Weekend

   _____

Helping Hands

Draw the hands on each clock to show the time.

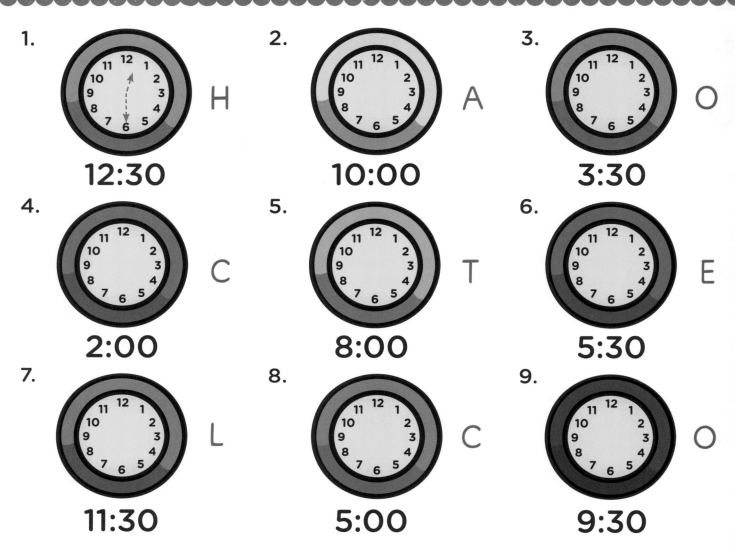

1. 12:30   H

2. 10:00   A

3. 3:30   O

4. 2:00   C

5. 8:00   T

6. 5:30   E

7. 11:30   L

8. 5:00   C

9. 9:30   O

Look at the arrows and find the clock above that matches.
Write the letter on the line to read the message.

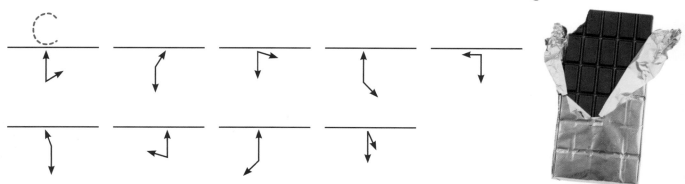

C

Short Stuff

An **abbreviation** is a shortened word. An abbreviation usually ends with a period. For example, the abbreviation for **August** is **Aug.** Some common abbreviations shorten the names of people, days, and months. Draw a line from each word to its abbreviation.

1. Missus
2. Mister
3. Doctor
4. Junior
5. Senior
6. Miss/Missus

Dr.
Ms.
Mr.
Sr.
Mrs.
Jr.

JUNE

SUN.	MON.	TUES.	WED.	THURS.	FRI.	SAT.
			1	2	3	4
5	6	7	8	9	10	11
12	13	14	15	16	17	18
19	20	21	22	23	24	25
26	27	28	29	30		

7. January
8. February
9. Tuesday
10. Thursday
11. August
12. Sunday
13. Saturday
14. September

Sat.
Jan.
Aug.
Feb.
Sun.
Tues.
Sept.
Thurs.

15. December
16. Monday
17. October
18. Wednesday
19. Friday
20. November
21. April
22. March

Wed.
Mon.
Dec.
Nov.
Mar.
Oct.
Fri.
Apr.

Dress for the Weather

Circle the names of clothes you would wear in each season.
Some clothes can be worn in more than one season.

Winter

(mittens)	coat
sandals	boots
shorts	T-shirt
sweater	skirt
wool hat	sunglasses

Spring

T-shirt	dress
tank top	mittens
sandals	raincoat
shorts	scarf
skirt	earmuffs

Summer

tank top	wool hat
earmuffs	shorts
sunglasses	sandals
gloves	T-shirt
dress	boots

Fall

coat	tank top
jeans	mittens
gloves	wool hat
sandals	sweater
scarf	swimsuit

Race Cars

Add the numbers to solve each problem.
Circle the car whose equations all have the same answer.

32 + 21	25 + 12	42 +36
40 + 13	80 + 19	14 + 64
10 +25	72 +24	53 +25

A Long Way to Go

Write the vowels to complete each word.

a__e	ai	ay	ee
ea	oa	ow	oe
o__e	ie	y	
i__e	ue	u__e	

1. r o s e

2. b__ __

3. r__ __n

4. p__ __

5. b__k__

6. t__ __

7. t__b__

8. cr__

9. gl__ __

10. b__ __t

11. h__ __

12. b__ __

13. c__k__

14. l__ __f

List the words from above under the correct vowel sound.

long a	long e	long i	long o	long u
_____	_____	_____	_____	_____
_____	_____	_____	_____	_____
_____		_____	_____	
			_____	

100 Chart

Can you count to 100? Fill in the missing numbers in the chart.
When you are done, count aloud **1** to **100**.

1	___	3	4	5	___	7	___	___	10
11	___	13	14	___	16	17	18	___	___
___	___	23	___	25	26	___	28	___	30
31	32	33	___	___	36	___	___	39	40
___	42	43	___	45	46	___	___	49	50
51	52	___	___	55	___	___	58	___	60
61	___	___	64	65	66	___	___	___	70
___	72	73	74	___	___	___	78	79	80
81	___	83	___	85	86	87	___	89	___
91	___	___	___	95	96	___	98	99	___

Number Fun

Complete the activity below.

Count by 2s. Write the missing numbers.

2	F _____	6	N _____	10
O _____	14	R _____	E _____	20
T _____	H _____	26	E _____	30

Count by 10s. Write the missing numbers.

10	20	I _____	S _____	50
U _____	T _____	80	90	100

Find each number above and write the letter to complete the joke.

Where did the numbers have a picnic?

I ___ ___ ___ ___
30 8   70 24 18

___ ___ ___ ___ ___ ___ ___
4   12 60 16 28 40 70

Bonnie's Boat Trip

Read the story. Then answer the questions.

Bonnie's boat slowly crept through the murky water. She paddled toward a shady tree to get out of the blazing sun. A snake dozed high in the tree's branches. Mosquitoes buzzed above the steamy water. Bonnie waited quietly in the thick, damp air. Suddenly, a scaly green tail flashed through the water. Bonnie got her camera ready. She had been waiting all day to get a picture of an alligator.

1. What is the setting?
   a) a forest
   b) a swamp
   c) a desert

2. What kinds of animals live here?

   _____

   _____

3. What is the weather like?

   _____

   _____

4. Draw a picture to show the setting of the story.

Bonnie · Boat · Trip · 59

Dollar Days

Circle the coins in each group that make exactly $1.00.

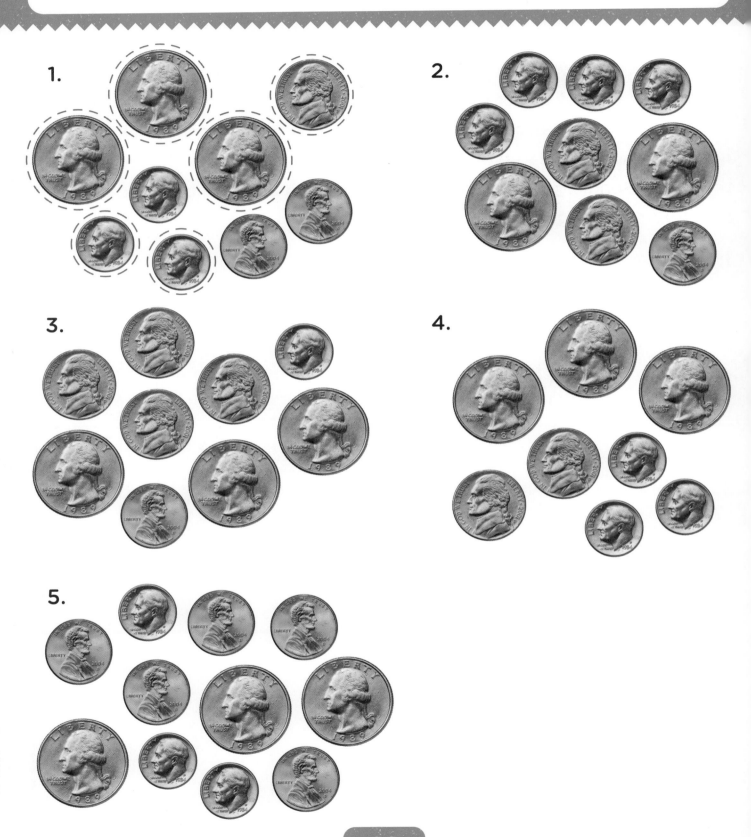

1.

2.

3.

4.

5.

Taking Sides

Count the number of sides and corners on each shape.
Circle the shape that does not belong.

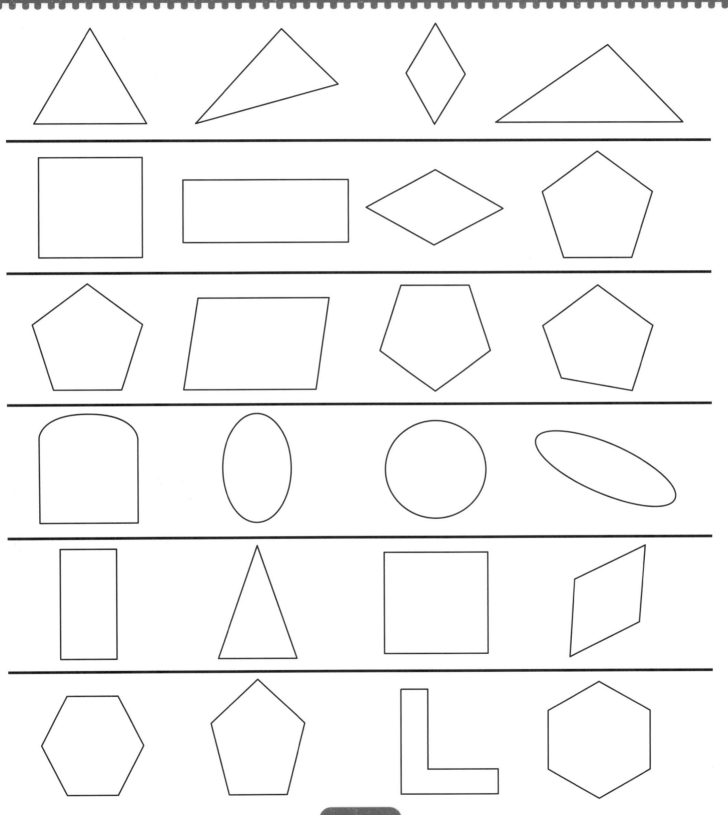

Putting It Together

Draw a line to connect each contraction with the two words it comes from.
Then complete the activity below.

can't	are not
won't	could not
isn't	will not
aren't	is not
couldn't	did not
didn't	can not

Underline the two words that can make a contraction.
Write the contraction on the line.

1. I <u>did not</u> wake up on time today. ___didn't___

2. I could not hear the alarm. _____

3. I can not be late to school. _____

4. My parents are not going to like this. _____

5. The bus is not going to wait. _____

6. I will not get to school on time! _____

Ending Sentences

Diffrerent kinds of sentences have different ending punctuation.

A **statement** ends with a period. (**.**)
A **question** ends with a question mark. (**?**)
An **exclamation** ends with an exclamation mark. (**!**)

Write the correct punctuation mark
at the end of each sentence in each paragraph.

1. Would you like to come with me to the store
I am going to buy new school clothes   I would like
to buy new shoes and a coat   After we shop, we can
go out to lunch   Do you want burgers or pizza

2. Mia and her friends were so excited   They
were going to the zoo   At the zoo, they saw all
kinds of wild animals   Which do you think was
Mia's favorite   Of all the animals, Mia liked the
giraffes the best

3. Daniel was nervous   Today was the first game
of the baseball playoffs   How many games had
the Tigers won this season   Daniel was proud
they had won all games but one   Oh no   It was
starting to rain   They would have to wait until
tomorrow to play

What Kind Is It?

There are three kinds of sentences.

A **declarative** sentence makes a statement. It ends with a period. (**.**)
The cat is on the bed.

An **exclamatory** sentence shows strong feeling or excitement.
It ends with an exclamation mark. (**!**)
Watch out for that ladder!

An **interrogative** sentence asks a question. It ends with a question mark. (**?**)
Do you want to go to the park?

What kinds of sentences are these? Write **D** for **declarative**,
E for **exclamatory**, or **I** for **interrogative**.

1. Did you buy milk at the store? _____ I

2. Justin won first place in the art contest. _____

3. I made my mom a special gift for her birthday. _____

4. Oh no, you stepped in the mud! _____

5. I'm so surprised! _____

6. Dad helped me with my math homework. _____

7. The lion roared loudly from the brush. _____

8. Which kitten would you like to take home? _____

9. Hurry, we'll be late for the bus! _____

10. How many stars can you count in the sky? _____

Figure It Out

Compare the numbers and the equations and write
< (less than), **>** (greater than), or **=** (equal to).

1.

3 [ ] 30

21 [ ] 21

44 [ ] 14

2.

10 [ ] 3 + 1

6 [ ] 5 + 4

8 [ ] 3 + 5

3.

2 + 1 [ ] 2 + 2

3 + 4 [ ] 6 + 0

2 + 8 [ ] 8 + 2

4.

7 + 1 [ ] 4 + 5

5 + 1 [ ] 3 + 3

4 + 2 [ ] 3 + 1

5.

5 - 3 [ ] 6 - 2

8 - 3 [ ] 7 - 5

6 - 3 [ ] 10 - 7

6.

8 - 7 [ ] 5 - 4

4 - 0 [ ] 7 - 4

8 - 8 [ ] 7 - 2

7.

1 + 4 [ ] 10 - 5

6 + 2 [ ] 6 - 3

2 + 0 [ ] 10 - 7

8.

10 - 4 [ ] 4 + 4

9 - 5 [ ] 2 + 2

6 - 1 [ ] 3 + 0

Action-Packed Party

Complete the activity below.

A **verb** is an action word.

She **blows** out the candles.

Circle the words that are verbs.

cake   sing   birthday   clap

party   candles   melt   blow

Now write some action words you see in the picture:

_____   _____   _____

Circle the verb in each sentence.

1. Molly closes her eyes.

2. Her friends shout, "Happy Birthday!"

3. Everyone eats a lot of cake.

4. Then Molly opens her gifts.

Order the Story

The events in a story are told in a certain order.
Put the sentences for each story in order by writing the numbers **1** to **4**.

1. _____ When she was clean, Shaggy jumped out of the tub.

   _____ Brandon put Shaggy in the soapy tub.

   _____ He washed Shaggy until she was squeaky-clean.

   _____ Shaggy dried off by shaking water all over Brandon.

2. _____ Tim kicked the winning goal.

   _____ The team celebrated and the crowd cheered.

   _____ Then he kicked the ball down the field.

   _____ Tim got the ball from a teammate.

3. _____ In the spring, Lan planted tomatoes.

   _____ She picked the ripe tomatoes and put them in a basket.

   _____ Lan gave bags of fresh tomatoes to her neighbors.

   _____ The tomato plants grew quickly.

4. _____ Jerome spread peanut butter on the bread.

   _____ Jerome felt hungry for a peanut butter sandwich.

   _____ He got some bread and peanut butter.

   _____ The sandwich was delicious.

Spell It Out

Solve each equation. Write the answer as a word in the puzzle.

Across

2. 5 + 1 = _____

3. 8 – 7 = _____

4. 10 – 2 = _____

6. 3 + 7 = _____

8. 11 – 6 = _____

Down

1. 9 – 7 = _____

2. 2 + 5 = _____

5. 9 – 6 = _____

7. 3 + 6 = _____

8. 12 – 8 = _____

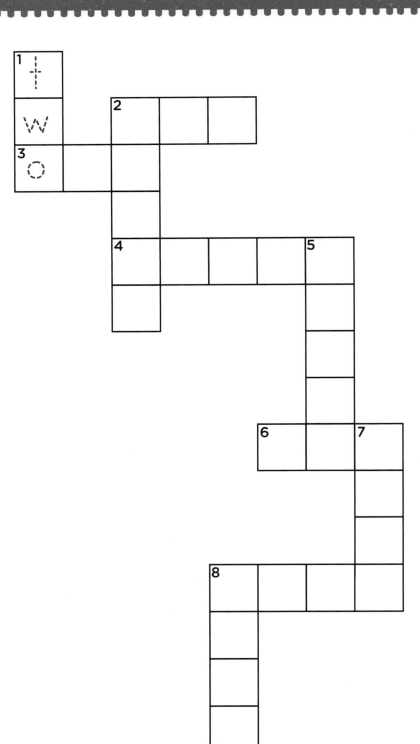

Read and Write

Choose a storybook from home or a library.
Read the book and answer the questions below.

Book title: _____

Author: _____

The story takes place in _____

The characters in the book are _____

_____

This is what happens in the story. First _____

_____

Then, _____

_____

Finally, _____

_____

My favorite part was when _____

_____

Now draw a picture of your favorite part.

All About America

Complete each sentence about American symbols.
Use the words in the word box to help you.

"The Star-Spangled Banner"   Capitol   bald eagle
Statue of Liberty   Liberty Bell   flag

1. This is the _Statue_
of Liberty.
It is a symbol of freedom.

2. This is a _____
_____.
It is our national bird.

3. This is the _____
_____.
It is a symbol of liberty.

4. This is the American
_____.
It has 50 stars and 13
red and white stripes.

5. The name of our national anthem is
_____.
Francis Scott Key wrote the words of the
anthem in 1814.

6. This is the United States
_____.
It is in Washington, D.C.

Ice Cream Party

Read the menu at the ice cream shop. Then solve the problems.

Single Scoop	25¢		Chocolate Sauce	15¢
Double Scoop	40¢		Caramel Sauce	15¢
Triple Scoop	55¢		Candy Sprinkles	10¢
Banana Split	$1.00		Cookie Bits	10¢
Chocolate Sundae	$1.00		Gummy Bears	5¢

1. Brad got a double scoop with chocolate sauce and cookie bits. How much did he spend? 40¢ + 15¢ + 10¢ = 65¢

2. Jacob got a single scoop with caramel sauce. How much did he spend?_____

3. Lauren got a chocolate sundae with extra candy sprinkles. How much did she spend?_____

4. Jamie got a triple scoop with caramel sauce and gummy bears. How much did he spend?_____

5. Mateo got a banana split with extra chocolate sauce. How much did he spend?_____

Rabbit Race

Subtract the numbers. Cross off each answer as you go.
See which bunny makes it all the way to the carrots!

| 13 | 32 | 42 | 81 | 16 |

| 22 | 52 | 11 | 70 | 61 |

1.
```
   17
 -  4
 ─────
   13
```

2.
```
   24
 -  2
 ─────
```

3.
```
   58
 -  6
 ─────
```

4.
```
   35
 -  3
 ─────
```

5.
```
   47
 -  5
 ─────
```

6.
```
   88
 -  7
 ─────
```

7.
```
   19
 -  8
 ─────
```

8.
```
   73
 -  3
 ─────
```

9.
```
   66
 -  5
 ─────
```

Rhyme and Riddle

Write two words that rhyme with the first word.
Then write the short or the long vowel below the words.

1. hat

bat

cat

short a

2. pen

_____

_____

3. sit

_____

_____

4. mop

_____

_____

5. mug

_____

_____

6. bake

_____

_____

7. heat

_____

_____

8. dine

_____

_____

9. rope

_____

_____

10. true

_____

_____

Solve each riddle with a rhyming word.

1. When you hike, be sure to pack
some water and a tasty _____.

2. The sun goes down. The time is soon
when you can see the stars and _____.

3. It's time for you to go to bed.
Lie down and rest your sleepy _____.

4. It's now time to clean up the room.
You'll need a dust pan and a _____.

Shape Puzzle

The numbers below are in a shape puzzle.
Use the shape around each number to solve the problems below.

2	8	5
7	3	1
4	6	9

For example:

⌐ = 9

⌐ + ☐ = 12

1. ⌐9 + 6⌐ + ⌐1 = 16

2. ⌐ + ☐ + ⌐ = ___

3. ∟ + ∟ + ☐ = ___

4. ☐ + ⌐ + ∟ = ___

5. ∟ + ∟ + ☐ = ___

6. ∟ + ∟ + ⌐ = ___

7. ☐ + ∟ + ⌐ = ___

8. ⌐ + ∟ + ☐ = ___

9. ∟ + ⌐ + ☐ = ___

10. ☐ + ☐ + ∟ = ___

11. ∟ + ∟ + ☐ = ___

12. ∟ + ⌐ + ∟ = ___

Funny Money

Connect the coin groups with equal value.

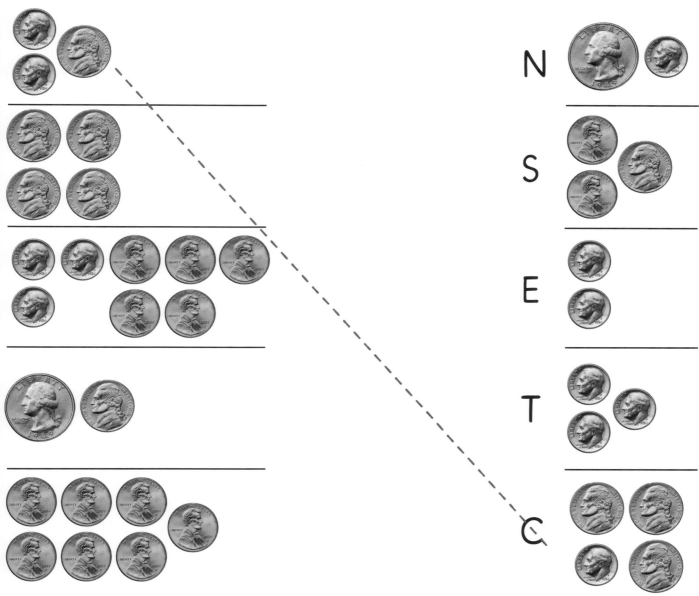

Find the coin groups that equal each amount.
Write the letter your line passed through.

Why did the boy lose his money?

Because he had no

C				
25¢	20¢	35¢	30¢	7¢

Bubble Fun

Read the story. Then answer the questions.

Bubbles are one of the most popular toys in the world. In fact, people buy 200 million bottles a year! You can make your own bubble solution at home. Pour one gallon of water into a large tub or tray. Then mix in $\frac{2}{3}$ cup dish detergent. You can use a can, a hanger, or even a hula hoop as your bubble wand. Dip it into the tray and wave it in the air to make giant bubbles.

1. How many bottles of bubbles are sold each year? _____

2. Circle the two ingredients you need to make a bubble solution.
   a) 1 gallon dish detergent
   b) $\frac{2}{3}$ cup dish detergent
   c) 1 gallon water
   d) 200 bubbles

3. Name three things you can use as a bubble wand.

   _____ _____ _____

4. Number the steps for making bubble solution at home.
   _____ Mix in $\frac{2}{3}$ cup of dish detergent
   _____ Pour a gallon of water into a large tray.
   _____ Wave it in the air.
   _____ Dip a can, a hanger, or a hula hoop into the mixture.

Secret Word

Look at the bold words in each sentence. Find the letter that is in the first two words, but not in the last word. Write that letter in the box. When you are done, read the letters from top to bottom. What is the secret word?

1. It is in **dig** and **hand**, but not **cat**.

   `d`

2. It is in **wild** and **pig**, but not in **laugh**.

3. It is in **name** and **knit**, but not in **baby**.

4. It is in **coat** and **oven**, but not in **car**.

5. It is in **wish** and **snake**, but not in **meat**.

6. It is in **wait** and **lamb**, but not in **dog**.

7. It is in **bump** and **huge**, but not in **love**.

8. It is in **rain** and **tire**, but not in **ice**.

What is the secret word? _____

Now draw a picture of the secret word.

In a Dictionary

In a dictionary, words are in alphabetical order. If words have the same first letter, look at the second letter. Write each group of words in alphabetical order.

1.
apple   always
ace   after

ace
after
always
apple

2.
book   brook
blank   ball

_____
_____
_____
_____

3.
creek   clown
cold   cave

_____
_____
_____
_____

4.
day   drain
dinner desk

_____
_____
_____
_____

5.
proud   plane
people pail

_____
_____
_____
_____

6.
rhino   raccoon
rust   roam

_____
_____
_____
_____

7.
story   slide
snake   sale

_____
_____
_____
_____

8.
trail   team
tool   tide

_____
_____
_____
_____

Swap and Subtract

Complete the activity below.

You can swap the numbers in an equation and get the same answer!

$$2 + 1 = 3 \longrightarrow 1 + 2 = 3$$

$$3 - 1 = 2 \longrightarrow 3 - 2 = 1$$

Fill in the missing numbers to solve the equations.

1. $4 + 2 =$ _____

    $2 +$ _____ $= 6$

    $6 - 2 =$ _____

    $6 -$ _____ $= 2$

2. $7 + 3 =$ _____

    $3 +$ _____ $= 10$

    $10 -$ _____ $= 3$

    $10 -$ _____ $= 7$

3. $4 + 8 =$ _____

    _____ $+ 4 = 12$

    $12 -$ _____ $= 8$

    _____ $- 8 = 4$

4. $3 +$ _____ $= 7$

    _____ $+$ _____ $= 7$

    $7 -$ _____ $= 3$

    _____ $-$ _____ $= 4$

5. $10 + 5 =$ _____

    $5 +$ _____ $=$ _____

    $15 -$ _____ $=$ _____

    _____ $- 10 =$ _____

6. $6 +$ _____ $= 11$

    _____ $+$ _____ $=$ _____

    _____ $-$ _____ $= 5$

    _____ $-$ _____ $=$ _____

Word Window

Find the word in each pair that is spelled correctly and circle it.

becuase
because

said
sead

befor
before

they
thay

once
wons

wer
were

our
uor

thare
there

pritty
pretty

Complete each sentence. Use a word from the window above.

1. We _____ playing baseball outside.

2. Then _____ ball broke a window.

3. "Oh, no!" we all _____.

4. We must pay for the window _____ we broke it.

In the Meadow

Read the paragraph. Then answer the questions.

I will never forget last summer. My family went on a camping trip to the mountains. We set up our tent next to a big, beautiful meadow. The meadow was filled with yellow flowers. Each night, I fell asleep to the sounds of croaking frogs and chirping crickets. One morning, I went for a walk in the meadow. I watched bees buzzing around the flowers. I felt the warm sun on my back. Then right in front of me, I saw a doe and her fawn. I stood without moving. I hoped they would stay, but they did not. They ran off into the woods. It lasted only a few moments. I will never forget the deer in the meadow.

1. When did my family go camping? _____

2. Where did my family go camping? _____

3. What filled the meadow? _____

_____

4. What special thing did I see in the meadow? _____

5. What sounds did I hear as I was falling alseep?

_____

_____

_____

Animal Groups

Animals belong to special groups.

Most **mammals** live on land. Most mammals are warm-blooded and have fur. Most give birth to live young.

Some **reptiles** live on land and some live in water. They are cold-blooded and have scales. Most of them lay eggs.

Fish live in water. Fish have scales and breathe through gills. Most lay eggs.

Birds live on land. Birds have feathers and wings, but not all can fly. They lay eggs.

Write these animal names in the correct column below.

chicken   rattlesnake   lizard   robin
alligator   eagle   monkey   dinosaur
catfish   deer   tuna   eel
skunk   parrot   trout   lion

MAMMALS	REPTILES	FISH	BIRDS
skunk			

Sign Search

Figure out whether the equation needs a plus or a minus sign.
Write **+** or **−** in each equation.

1.

$3 \boxed{} 4 = 7$

$8 \boxed{} 4 = 4$

2.

$10 \boxed{} 1 = 11$

$10 \boxed{} 5 = 5$

3.

$8 \boxed{} 3 = 5$

$9 \boxed{} 4 = 13$

4.

$6 \boxed{} 7 = 13$

$16 \boxed{} 8 = 8$

5.

$5 \boxed{} 9 = 14$

$9 \boxed{} 7 = 2$

6.

$9 \boxed{} 8 = 17$

$5 \boxed{} 4 = 1$

7.

$12 \boxed{} 7 = 5$

$8 \boxed{} 7 = 15$

8.

$13 \boxed{} 3 = 10$

$3 \boxed{} 7 = 10$

Dressed to Describe

Complete the activity below.

An **adjective** describes something.

Sarah is wearing a **bright** outfit.

Circle the words that are adjectives.

dress	big	floppy	hold
shiny	wear	hat	hungry

Fill in the adjectives to describe what you see in the picture.

_____ dress   _____ shoes   _____ hat

Circle the adjectives that describe what you see in the picture.

1. Look at Sarah's pretty outfit.

2. Her dress has big flowers on it.

3. She wears a floppy hat.

4. It sits on her long hair.

Manners Matter

Good manners help people get along with each other. Complete each sentence with a word from the box. Use your answers to complete the crossword puzzle.

love

thank you

sorry

shake

may

open

smile

please

nice

excuse

1 Across: t h a n k y o u

Across

1. When you recieve a gift, you say, "_____."
4. It is polite to _____ the door for people.
7. When you ask a favor, you always say, "_____."
9. When you are asking permission to do something, say, "_____I?"

Down

2. When you meet someone, you say, "_____ to meet you."
3. When you do something wrong, you say, "I'm _____."
5. When you need to get by someone, you say, "_____ me."
6. People like to see a friendly _____ on your face.
8. Say "I _____ you" to the people you care about.
10. When you meet people, it is polite to _____ their hand.

Time Match Up

There are different ways to write time.

2:15
quarter past 2
15 minutes after 2

Draw lines to match the times in all three columns.

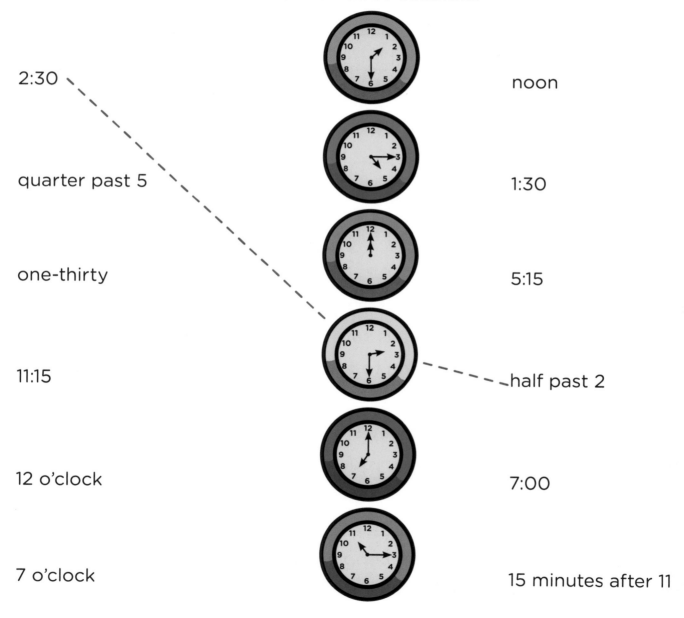

2:30

quarter past 5

one-thirty

11:15

12 o'clock

7 o'clock

noon

1:30

5:15

half past 2

7:00

15 minutes after 11

Food for Thought

Complete the activity below.

My favorite food is a peanut butter sandwich. The light brown bread feels soft. The peanut butter looks like thick frosting. It smells like fresh roasted peanuts and tastes creamy.

Now draw a picture of your favorite food.
Complete the sentences to write a descriptive paragraph.

My favorite food is _____.

It looks like _____.

When I touch it, it feels _____.

I can smell _____.

It tastes so _____.

Estimation Station

An estimation is a guess based on what you know.
Estimate the price for each item. Circle your answer.

1.

($40) $400

2.

$7.50   75¢

3.

$1.50 $10.50

4.

$12 $120

5.

$15,000 $50

6.

$35 $3

7.

$500 $5

8.

$10 $1

Favorite Cookies

Look at the graph. Then answer the questions.

Number of Children

	Peanut Butter	Chocolate Chip	Sugar	Mint	Oatmeal
6					
5				■	
4	■				
3	■			■	■
2	■		■	■	■
1	■		■	■	■

Kinds of Cookies

1. Which cookie do children like best? _chocolate chip_

2. Which cookie do children like least? _____

3. How many children like mint cookies? _____

4. How many more children like chocolate chip cookies than sugar cookies?

   _____

5. Do more children like peanut butter cookies or oatmeal cookies?

   _____

Road Race

Solve the equations. Find the answer and cross it out.
See which car wins the race!

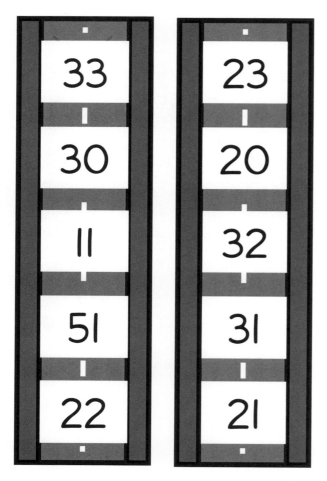

33		23	
30		20	
11		32	
51		31	
22		21	

1.
$$\begin{array}{r} 55 \\ -\ 22 \\ \hline 33 \end{array}$$

2.
$$\begin{array}{r} 34 \\ -\ 11 \\ \hline \end{array}$$

3.
$$\begin{array}{r} 76 \\ -\ 46 \\ \hline \end{array}$$

4.
$$\begin{array}{r} 28 \\ -\ 17 \\ \hline \end{array}$$

5.
$$\begin{array}{r} 40 \\ -\ 20 \\ \hline \end{array}$$

6.
$$\begin{array}{r} 89 \\ -\ 57 \\ \hline \end{array}$$

7.
$$\begin{array}{r} 93 \\ -\ 42 \\ \hline \end{array}$$

8.
$$\begin{array}{r} 62 \\ -\ 31 \\ \hline \end{array}$$

9.
$$\begin{array}{r} 39 \\ -\ 17 \\ \hline \end{array}$$

10.
$$\begin{array}{r} 51 \\ -\ 30 \\ \hline \end{array}$$

S Starters

Write the blend to complete each word. Use each blend twice.

| sk | sl | sn | sm | sp | st |

____op

____unk

____ake

____oon

____eep

____ar

____oke

____ide

____ill

____ail

____ell

____ate

List the words from above under the correct blend.

sk	sl	sn	sm	sp	st
_____	_____	_____	_____	_____	_____
_____	_____	_____	_____	_____	_____

Solve the Riddle

Look at the bold words in each sentence. Find the letter that is in the first two words, but not in the last word. Write that letter in the box. When you are done, read the letters from top to bottom. If you are correct, you will solve the riddle.

The more of them you take, the more you leave behind.
Write the letters on the lines below.

1. It is in **frog** and **fan** but not in **sit**. `f`

2. It is in **hop** and **cot** but not in **ace**.

3. It is in **mop** and **boat** but not in **kite**.

4. It is in **tan** and **top** but not in **mud**.

5. It is in **sit** and **ask** but not in **me**.

6. It is in **bat** and **ten** but not in **dog**.

7. It is in **eel** and **eat** but not in **soap**.

8. It is in **pin** and **map** but not in **bed**.

9. It is in **sea** and **sun** but not in **wet**.

Answer:

___ ___   ___   ___   ___   ___   ___   ___   ___

Just Joking

Add or subtract. Then answer the question below.

1. $\begin{array}{r} 44 \\ -33 \\ \hline \end{array}$ S	2. $\begin{array}{r} 25 \\ +22 \\ \hline \end{array}$ S	3. $\begin{array}{r} 63 \\ -43 \\ \hline \end{array}$ E	4. $\begin{array}{r} 51 \\ -21 \\ \hline \end{array}$ S
5. $\begin{array}{r} 51 \\ +36 \\ \hline \end{array}$ T	6. $\begin{array}{r} 96 \\ -62 \\ \hline \end{array}$ N	7. $\begin{array}{r} 38 \\ -17 \\ \hline \end{array}$ N	8. $\begin{array}{r} 17 \\ +62 \\ \hline \end{array}$ I
9. $\begin{array}{r} 58 \\ +31 \\ \hline \end{array}$ H	10. $\begin{array}{r} 84 \\ -71 \\ \hline \end{array}$ O	11. $\begin{array}{r} 77 \\ +21 \\ \hline \end{array}$ E	

Find each number above and write the letter to answer the joke.

What kind of shoes do numbers wear?

$\underline{\text{I}}\ \underline{\quad}\ \underline{\quad}\ \underline{\quad}\ \underline{\quad}\ \underline{\quad}$
87   20   34   21   79   47

$\underline{\quad}\ \underline{\quad}\ \underline{\quad}\ \underline{\quad}\ \underline{\quad}$
11   89   13   98   30

Book Basics

Look at the table of contents. Then answer the questions.

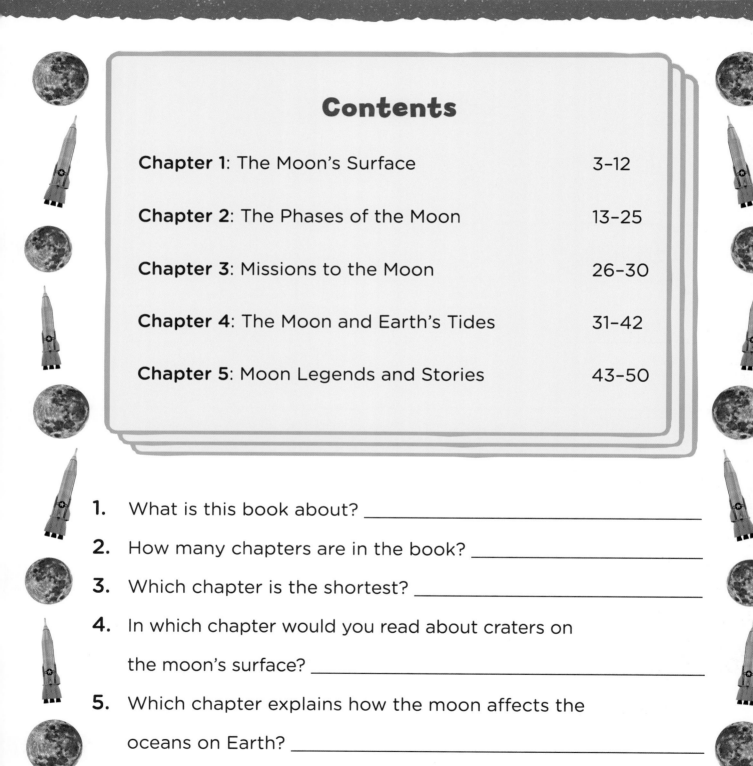

Contents

1. What is this book about? _____

2. How many chapters are in the book? _____

3. Which chapter is the shortest? _____

4. In which chapter would you read about craters on
    the moon's surface? _____

5. Which chapter explains how the moon affects the
    oceans on Earth? _____

Going Places

Write the name of each vehicle under the picture.
Use the words in the box to help you.

helicopter	sailboat	car	truck
airplane	train	bicycle	ship
hot air balloon	motorcycle	scooter	skateboard

1.

_____car_____

2.

_____

3.

_____

4.

_____

5.

_____

6.

_____

7.

_____

8.

_____

9.

_____

10.

_____

11.

_____

12.

_____

Can You Buy It?

Look at the price of each item and count the coins.
If you have enough money to buy it, circle **Yes**. If not, circle **No**.

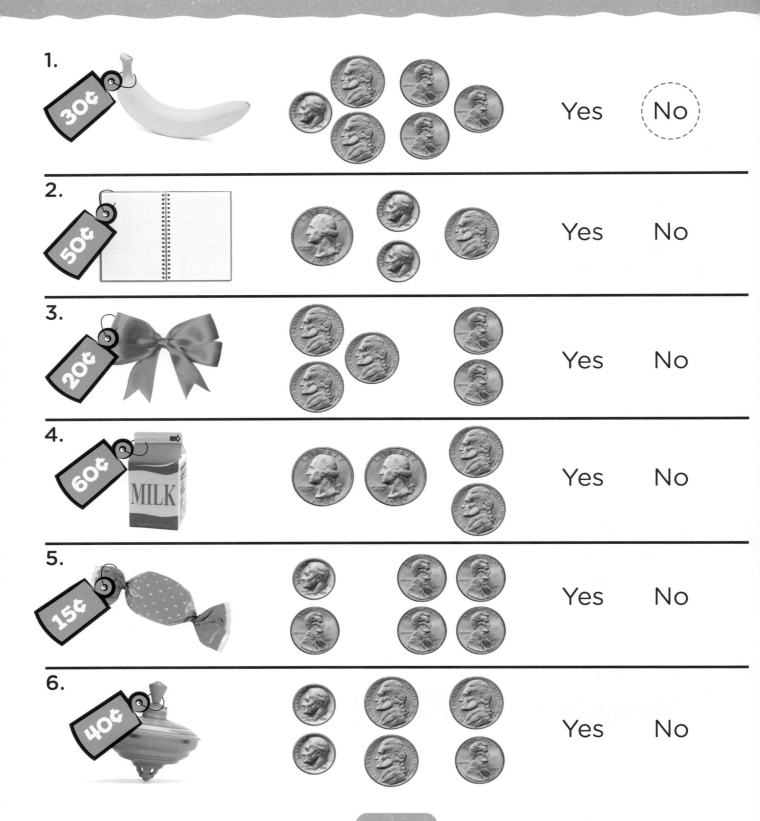

1. 30¢   Yes   No

2. 50¢   Yes   No

3. 20¢   Yes   No

4. 60¢   Yes   No

5. 15¢   Yes   No

6. 40¢   Yes   No

Short Cuts

Draw a line to connect each abbreviation with its matching word.

Dr.	Street
Jan.	Mister
St.	Doctor
Sun.	December
Dec.	Missus
Mr.	January
Ave.	Sunday
Mrs.	Avenue

Write each date using abbreviations.

1. Monday, February 6   *Mon., Feb. 6*

2. Tuesday, November 10   _____

3. Friday, October 2   _____

4. Saturday, August 8   _____

Mixing Colors

If you mix certain colors, you can make new colors! See how many new colors you can make by solving each color problem. Color the shape the new color.

1.

blue + yellow = __green__

2.

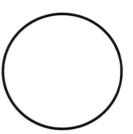

red + white = _____

3.

red + blue = _____

4.

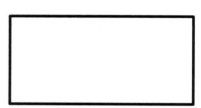

red + yellow = _____

5.

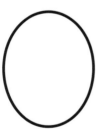

black + white = _____

6. Now, mix your own two colors! write the colors below then color the star your new color.

_____ + _____ = _____

Soccer Sentences

Complete the activity below.

Use capitals for:

- First word of a sentence
- Days of the week
- Months
- Titles like Mr. and Mrs.
- People's names

Every **S**aturday in **J**une, **M**rs. **J**ones coaches soccer.

Rewrite each sentence with correct capitalization. Don't forget to capitalize the first word in the sentence, the word "I," and people's names.

1. on mondays i have soccer practice.

   On Mondays I have soccer practice.

2. my coach is mrs. jones.

   _____

3. every thursday we have a soccer game.

   _____

4. our soccer team plays in april and may.

   _____

5. in june there is a big game to end the season.

   _____

6. even mr. jones comes to cheer on the team.

   _____

Sharing with Friends

Fractions help you divide things into equal parts.
Draw lines to divide each food into equal parts. Write the fraction.

1 whole = 2 halves ($\frac{1}{2}$)
(2 equal pieces)

1 whole = 4 fourths ($\frac{1}{4}$)
(4 equal pieces)

1.

Divide into 4 equal pieces.

Each piece = $\frac{1}{4}$

2.

Divide into 2 equal pieces.

Each piece = _____

3.

Divide into 2 equal pieces.

Each piece = _____

4.

Divide into 4 equal pieces.

Each piece = _____

5.

Divide into 2 equal pieces.

Each piece = _____

6.

Divide into 4 equal pieces.

Each piece = _____

Tic Tac Toe

Solve each problem. Find the row that has three equal answers, and circle it.

1. Jill has five tulips, and Jon has six roses. How many flowers do they have altogether?

_____ flowers

2. Ethan kicked five goals at the game, and so did Bruce. How many goals did they kick together?

_____ goals

3. Betty had twelve carrots. She gave six to Fran. How many carrots does Betty have left?

_____ carrots

4. Tom has two ladybugs, three beetles, and one cricket in his bug collection. How many bugs are there altogether?

_____ bugs

5. Brian had fifteen pieces of candy. He gave five to his brother. How many does he have left?

_____ pieces

6. The giant ice cream cone has two scoops of vanilla, two scoops of chocolate, and one scoop of strawberry. How many scoops does it have in total?

_____ scoops

7. Lynn had sixteen stickers in her collection. She gave eight to Nora. How many stickers does Lynn have left?

_____ stickers

8. Drew scored seven points during the game. Then he scored three more during overtime. How many points in total did he score?

_____ points

9. Dave has ten fingers and ten toes. How many fingers and toes does he have altogether?

_____ fingers and toes

Pen Pals

Think about something fun you've done this summer.
Draw a picture of what you did.

Now write a letter to a friend or family member
by completing the sentences below.

Dear _____,

This summer, I went to _____.

While I was there I saw _____ and

_____.

I did some fun things, like _____. I also

_____.

My favorite part was when we _____.

I will always remember this summer because

_____.

Your friend,

_____

Tools of the Trade

We use different tools to measure weight, length, temperature, and volume. Look at these measuring tools below. Then write which tool you would use to measure each item.

thermometer   measuring cup   scale   ruler

---

1. Amount of flour to add to cookie batter

   Tool: <u>measuring cup</u>

2. Your body temperature

   Tool: _____

3. Length of a room

   Tool: _____

4. Your height

   Tool: _____

5. Weight of tomatoes at the market

   Tool: _____

6. Amount of oatmeal to add to boiling water

   Tool: _____

7. Width of a doorway

   Tool: _____

8. Weight of a chicken

   Tool: _____

Following Directions

Directions must be written in a certain order to make sense.
Write numbers 1 to 5 to put each set of directions in the correct order.

1. _____ Put a pot of water on the stove to boil.

   _____ Pour the tomato sauce over cooked pasta.

   _____ Put the pasta in the boiling water.

   _____ As pasta is cooking, heat up tomato sauce.

   _____ Drain the pasta, and put it in a bowl.

   What did you make? _____

2. _____ Put your toothbrush away.

   _____ Rinse off your toothbrush.

   _____ Brush your teeth.

   _____ Take out your toothbrush and toothpaste.

   _____ Put toothpaste on your toothbrush.

   What did you do? _____

3. _____ Open the jam jar.

   _____ Put bread in the toaster.

   _____ Spread jam on the toasted bread.

   _____ Take out bread, jam, and a knife.

   _____ Take bread out of the toaster.

   What did you make? _____

Place Race

Count the groups of tens and ones, and write each number in standard form. Find each number on the path and cross it out. See which runner finishes first!

A

B

1.

2 tens + 4 ones = _24_

2.

3 tens + 4 ones = _____

3.

4 tens + 5 ones = _____

4.

5 tens + 4 ones = _____

5.

= _____

6.
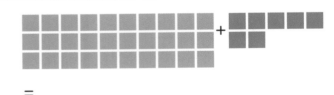

= _____

---

7. 4 tens + 8 ones = _____

8. 7 tens + 3 ones = _____

---

9. 8 tens + 6 ones = _____

10. 6 tens + 8 ones = _____

Beginning Blends

Write the blend to complete each word. Use each blend once.

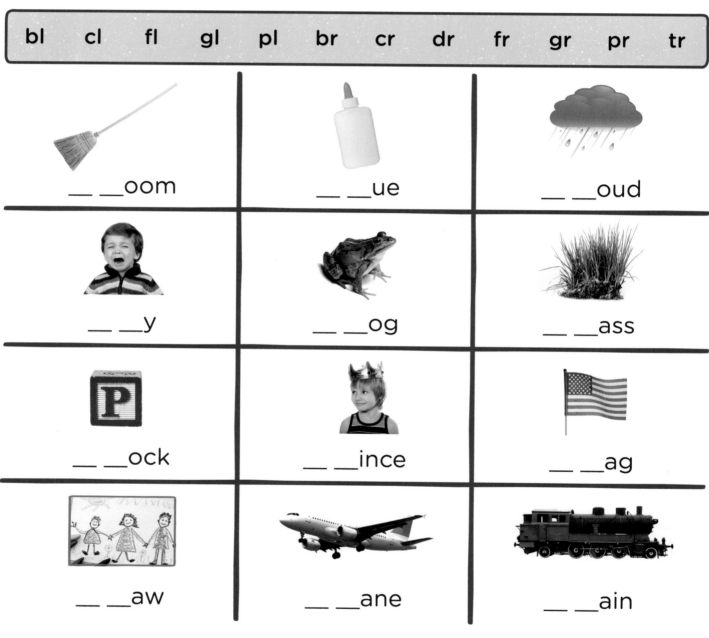

| bl | cl | fl | gl | pl | br | cr | dr | fr | gr | pr | tr |

__ __oom

__ __ue

__ __oud

__ __y

__ __og

__ __ass

__ __ock

__ __ince

__ __ag

__ __aw

__ __ane

__ __ain

Draw a line to connect the rhyming words.

plain   cry   blow   glass   press   free

fly   grow   tree   brain   class   dress

Contraction Action

A **contraction** is a short word made up of two other words.
The missing letter or letters are replaced with an apostrophe (').

I + am = I'm   did + not = didn't   will not = won't

Draw a line to match each contraction to the two words it is made from.

can't   I am

we'll   can not

they're   she is

don't   he is

I'm   they are

he's   we will

I'll   I will

she's   do not

The Amazing Kangaroo

Read about kangaroos. Then answer the questions.

When people think of Australia, they often think of kangaroos. Kangaroos are amazing animals. They use their powerful hind legs to jump great lengths. They can jump the length of a school bus! Kangaroos belong to a special group of animals called marsupials. Marsupials carry their babies in pouches. Baby kangaroos have a special name, too. They are called joeys. When a joey is born, it is only the size of a single pea. This tiny newborn stays in its mother's pouch for up to ten months. Then it comes out to explore the world. Even when a joey is too big for its mother's pouch, it will jump back in if it is scared!

1. Where do kangaroos live? _____Australia_____

2. To what group of animals do kangaroos belong? _____

3. Finish this sentence:

   Marsupials carry their babies in _____.

4. What is a baby kangaroo called? _____

5. How long does a baby kangaroo stay in its mother's pouch?

   _____

Addition Antics

Use regrouping to add.

1.   14
    + 6
    20
 	
     D
	2. 16
	    + 5
	
	     R
		3. 28
		    + 4
		
		     E
			4. 19
			    + 4
			
			     I

5.   25
    + 5
 	
     D
	6. 37
	    + 7
	
	     A
		7. 36
		    + 6
		
		     I
			8. 46
			    + 4
			
			     M

Find each number above and write the letter to complete the joke.

What did the number write on the valentine card?

<u> I </u>   _____   _____   _____   _____   _____   _____   _____   YOU!
 23   44   30   20   50   42   21   32

Our National Anthem

Read the story. Then look at each sentence below and circle **true** or **false**.

Francis Scott Key lived during the time of the Revolutionary War. One night, he was on a ship in the Baltimore Harbor. The British came to Fort McHenry that night. Francis watched the battle all night. In the morning, there was lots of smoke, but Francis could still see the American flag flying. He wrote a poem about the flag. The poem later became the song "The Star-Spangled Banner." Francis Scott Key helped give America this important song!

1. Francis Scott Key's poem became the song "The Star Spangled Banner."   True   False

2. Francis fought at Fort McHenry when the British came.   True   False

3. Francis watched the soldiers fighting all night long.   True   False

4. In the morning, Francis could see only smoke.   True   False

5. The song "The Star Spangled Banner" is about the flag.   True   False

Life Cycle of a Butterfly

The life cycle of a butterfly has four stages.
Write **1** to **4** to put the stages in order.

_____ **Caterpillar**: This plump creature eats and eats.
It splits and sheds its skin many times.

_____ **Butterfly**: This pretty insect comes out of the
pupa, totally changed.

_____ **Pupa**: The caterpillar attaches itself
to a plant and forms a hard shell.

_____ **Egg**: A female butterfly lays an egg on a plant
and leaves it to hatch.

Fill in the life cycle below. Draw and label a picture of each stage.

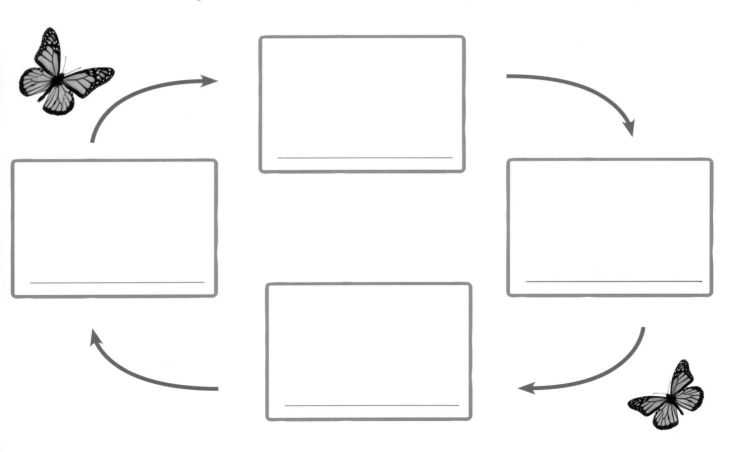

In My Community

Many people in our communities are there to help us. Fill in the community helper from the word box to complete each sentence.

police officer	firefighter	nurse	veterinarian	teacher
mail carrier	clerk	doctor	bus driver	dentist

1. A __firefighter__ rescues people and puts out fires.

2. At school, my _____ shows me how to read and write.

3. The _____ delivers mail to my home.

4. When my pet is sick, I take it to a _____.

5. When I am sick or need a checkup, I go see my _____.

6. At the market, the _____ helps me find and buy food.

7. The _____ takes me to school on the bus.

8. My _____ helps me keep my teeth healthy.

9. A _____ helps a doctor in many ways.

10. A _____ fights crime and helps me stay safe.

On a separate piece of paper, draw a picture of your favorite community helper. Show this person doing his or her job.

What's Your Favorite Meal?

Ask ten people what their favorite meal of the day is. Color in the rectangles to show how many people chose each meal. Start coloring at the bottom. Then answer the questions below.

10			
9			
8			
7			
6			
5			
4			
3			
2			
1			

breakfast   **lunch**   **dinner**

1. What is this graph about? _____

2. Which meal did the most people like? _____

3. Which meal did the fewest people like? _____

4. How many people said lunch was their favorite meal? _____

Puzzling Plurals

Write the plural for each word.

To show more than one, drop the letter **y** and add the letters **ies**.

 cherr~~y~~   cherr**ies**

1.

   pony   _____

2.

   baby   _____

3.

   berry   _____

4.

   daddy   _____

Circle the correct plural for each word.

5. **man**   a) mans   b) men   c) mens

6. **foot**   a) footes   b) foots   c) feet

7. **mouse**   a) mice   b) mouses   c) mousies

8. **tooth**   a) tooths   b) teeth   c) toothes

Morning, Afternoon, and Night

People usually do things during certain times of the day or night.
Circle **morning**, **afternoon**, or **night** to tell when you do each activity below.

1. I eat dinner.   morning   afternoon   night

2. I get home from school.   morning   afternoon   night

3. I leave for school.   morning   afternoon   night

4. I eat breakfast.   morning   afternoon   night

5. I go to sleep.   morning   afternoon   night

6. I eat lunch.   morning   afternoon   night

7. I take a bath.   morning   afternoon   night

8. I put on my pajamas.   morning   afternoon   night

Tell the Time

Write the time below each clock.

 (15 min)

To show 15 minutes past the hour, the big hand points to the 3.

(45 min)  (15 min)

(30 min)

To show 45 minutes past the hour, the big hand points to the 9. The little hand is almost pointing to the next number.

1.

2:15

2.

_____

3.

_____

4.

_____

5.

_____

6.

_____

Sam and Pam

Complete the activity below.

Possessives show something belongs to someone:

The cap belongs to Pam.
Pam**'s** cap

Pronouns stand in place of names.

He   She   They   It

Sam is a boy. **He** likes music.

Based on the pictures, write who it belongs to. Then write the possessive.

1. The piano belongs to ___Sam___.   ___Sam's___ piano

2. The bat belongs to _____.   _____ bat

3. The baseball belongs to _____.   _____ baseball

4. The music belongs to _____.   _____ music

Circle the person's name. Then circle the pronoun.
Write who the pronoun stands for.

5. (Sam) plays the piano.
    (He) likes music.
    ___Sam___

6. Pam plays baseball.
    She likes sports.
    _____

7. Sam and Pam are friends.
    They like to play.
    _____

8. Sam is cold.
    He is wearing a sweater.
    _____

Shop 'Til You Drop

Read each story problem below. Then circle **Yes** or **No** to answer the question.

1. The baseball costs 75¢. You have:

Do you have enough money?

(Yes)   No

2. The candy costs 60¢. You have:

Do you have enough money?

Yes   No

3. The popcorn costs 40¢. You have:

Do you have enough money?

Yes   No

4. The flowers costs 99¢. You have:

Do you have enough money?

Yes   No

5. The hamburger costs 57¢. You have:

Do you have enough money?

Yes   No

6. The doll costs 85¢. You have:

Do you have enough money?

Yes   No

Ring Toss

Figure out the number pattern in each row. Continue the pattern and fill in the empty rings with the last two numbers. Use the rings at the bottom for help.

| 2 | 4 | 6 | 8 | 10 | 12 |

| 5 | 10 | 15 | 20 | | |

| 1 | 3 | 5 | 7 | | |

| 3 | 6 | 9 | 12 | | |

| 4 | 8 | 12 | 16 | | |

30   10   12   20   11

9   18   24   15   25

Practice Time

Practice writing the letters in cursive.

Aa   Aa

Bb   Bb

Cc   Cc

Dd   Dd

Ee   Ee

Ff   Ff

Gg   Gg

Hh   Hh

Ii   Ii

Now practice writing your name in cursive.

Zoo Mix-Up

These zoo animals' names are all mixed up!
Unscramble the letters to spell each animal's name correctly.

1. e r b a   bear

2. a a k o l   _____

3. i r a g f e f   _____

4. h i r n o   _____

5. t g i r e   _____

6. b z r a e   _____

7. n s a e k   _____

8. e h l e a p t n   _____

9. n p e g u n i   _____

10. o n l i   _____

11. y m n k o e   _____

12. p i h p o   _____

BONUS WORD
Can you figure out this animal?

l i g a l a r t o

_____

Delightful Descriptions

Good writing has good descriptions. **Adjectives** are describing words.
Write three adjectives to describe each picture below. Try to use the best words you can.

soft
playful
cute

_____
_____
_____

_____
_____
_____

_____
_____
_____

_____
_____
_____

_____
_____
_____

Phonics Fun

Write the blend to complete each word. Use each blend three times.

ch	sh	th	wh

1.

__ __ip

2.

__ __eel

3.

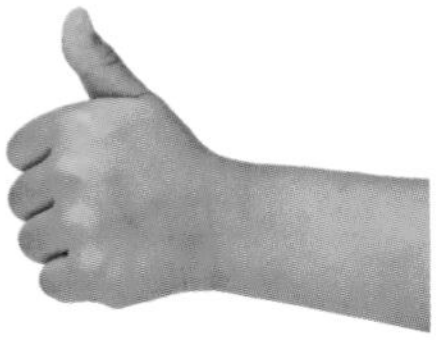

__ __umb

4.

__ __ree

5.

__ __istle

6.

__ __oe

7.

__ __air

8.

__ __in

9.

__ __eese

10.

__ __eek

11.

__ __ell

12.

__ __ale

List the words from above under the correct blend.

ch	sh	th	wh
_____	_____	_____	_____
_____	_____	_____	_____
_____	_____	_____	_____

Precious Pets

Owning a pet is a big responsibility. Pets need many things to live long and happy lives. Unscramble the word in each sentence to tell how you should care for a pet. Write the word on the line.

1. Give your pet a **T B H A** to keep it clean.

    bath

2. Make sure your pet gets its shots from the **T V E**.

    _____

3. Give your pet fresh **T R W A E** every day.

    _____

4. Some pets enjoy **A L W K S** for exercise.

    _____

5. Pets need good **O F O D** to stay strong and healthy.

    _____

6. Make time to have fun and **A P L Y** with your pet.

    _____

7. Most of all, give your pet lots of care and **V E O L**.

    _____

Find and circle the words above in the word search.
Words can go across or down.

P	L	A	Y	U	W	A
F	O	N	W	F	A	R
A	V	L	P	O	L	W
V	E	T	B	O	K	U
R	E	M	A	D	S	E
E	W	A	T	E	R	T
S	O	T	H	A	C	H

Let's Celebrate!

All families celebrate special events and holidays. In the quilt below, draw four pictures of special times or celebrations you shared with your family. Think of holidays, birthdays, parties, and more! Label each picture. Then color the quilt.

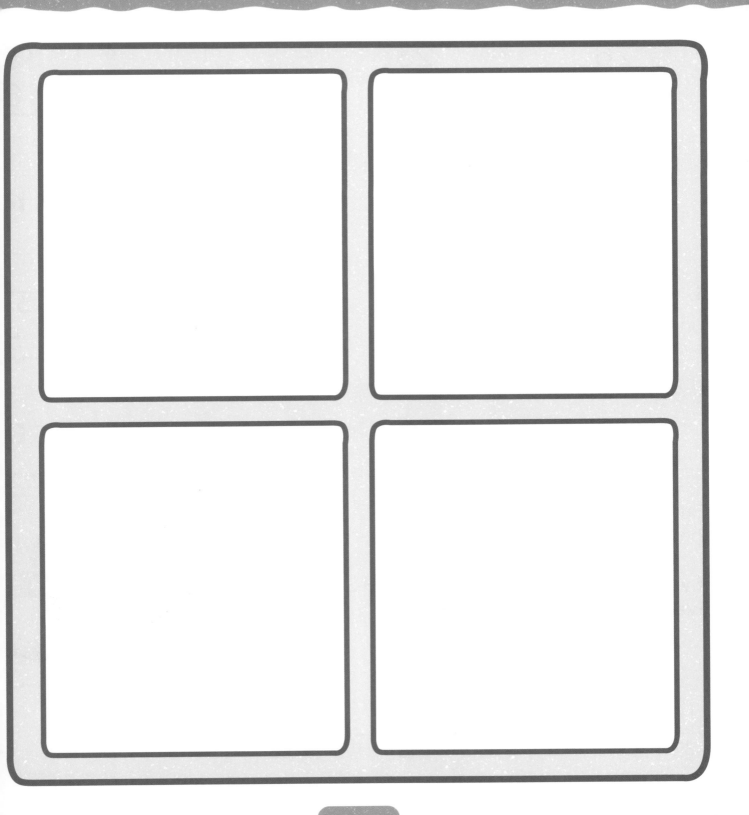

Laugh It Off

Use regrouping to subtract.

1.
```
  26
-  9
─────
  17
```
I

2.
```
  23
-  5
─────
```
A

3.
```
  31
-  8
─────
```
H

4.
```
  35
-  6
─────
```
N

5.
```
  44
-  7
─────
```
B

6.
```
  22
-  6
─────
```
G

7.
```
  46
-  8
─────
```
S

8.
```
  31
-  5
─────
```
D

Find each number above and write the letter to complete the joke.

If you have seven apples in one hand and five in the other, what do you have?

B __ __ __ __ __ __ __ !
37 17 16   23 18 29 26 38

A Dog's Day

Read the story. Then answer the questions.

Dogs are fun to play catch with or to curl up with on the couch. Yet having a pet dog isn't all fun and games. It's a lot of hard work, too.

A pet dog relies on its owner for food, water, and exercise every day. Someone has to fill the food bowl and take the dog for walks. Dogs also need checkups at a vet and shots to stay healthy.

A pet dog can be a special friend if you are ready for the responsibilities.

1. What is the main idea of the passage?

   a) Playing catch with a dog can be a lot of fun.
   b) Owning a dog comes with many responsibilities.

2. What is the author's purpose?

   a) To prove that having a pet dog is hard work.
   b) To inform the reader about what dogs eat.

3. List some of the things a dog owner must do.

   _____

   _____

   _____

4. Would you like to have a pet dog? Why or why or not?

   _____

   _____

   _____

Riddle Fun

Write the answer to the problem in each box. Then use the Answer Key to find the letter that matches the answer. Write the letter on the line below to answer the riddle.

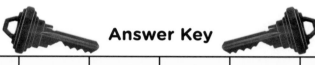 **Answer Key**

1	2	3	4	5	6	7	8	9	10
D	K	R	U	T	O	E	Y	N	M

Name three keys that don't unlock doors.

15 - 5	14 - 8	13 - 4	8 - 6	12 - 5	10 - 2
10					

M _____ _____ _____ _____ _____

8 - 3	10 - 6	11 - 8	9 - 7	8 - 1	14 - 6

_____ _____ _____ _____ _____ _____

6 - 5	11 - 5	16 - 7	5 - 3	14 - 7	13 - 5

_____ _____ _____ _____ _____ _____

It's About Time

Figure out how much time passed, and write it on the line.

1.   = 2 hours

2.   = _____

3.   = _____

Draw the hands to show the start and the finish times.

START  Jon started his test at 10:00.
He finished 30 minutes later.  FINISH

START  The game started at 2:15.
It finished 2 hours later.  FINISH

START  Meg's party started at 11:30.
It finished 3 hours later.  FINISH

Say It Again

Synonyms are words that mean almost the same thing.
Connect each word with its synonym.

1.	little	speedy	4.	laugh	mad
2.	run	jog	5.	angry	glad
3.	fast	small	6.	happy	giggle

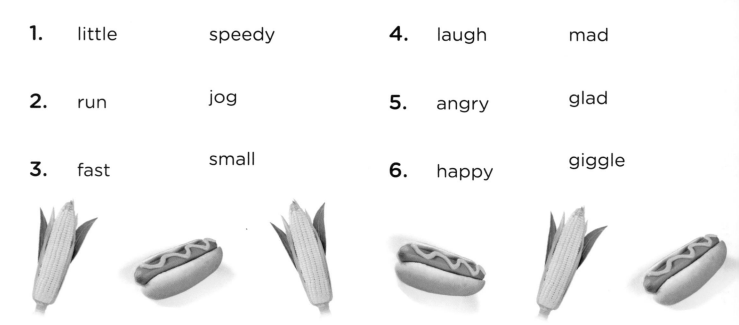

Look at the underlined word in each sentence. Find the word in the box that means almost the same thing. Write it on the line.

chatted	tasty	cooked	cold	feast

7. My whole family got together for a <u>barbecue</u>. _feast_

8. We <u>roasted</u> hot dogs over a fire. _____

9. The corn on the cob was so <u>yummy</u>! _____

10. The root beer was <u>chilled</u>. _____

11. I <u>talked</u> with my cousins. _____

Before and After

Complete the activity below.

Fill in the missing numbers by counting forward.

1. 33 __34__ 35

2. 29 _____ 31

3. 54 55 _____

4. 16 _____ _____ 19

5. 48 _____ 50 _____

6. 32 33 _____ _____

7. 96 _____ 98 _____ _____

8. 61 62 _____ _____ _____

Fill in the missing numbers by counting backward.

9. 67 __66__ 65

10. 90 91 _____

11. 20 _____ 18

12. 72 71 _____ _____

13. 80 _____ _____ 77

14. 57 _____ 55 _____

15. 29 _____ _____ 26 _____

16. 44 _____ 42 _____ _____

Scrambled Sentences

Unscramble the words and write the sentence.

1. camped lake . the I at

   _____

2. up tent . We put a

   _____

3. bag . I in slept sleeping a

   _____

4. . over fire We a cooked

   _____

5. fishing I went the . lake in

   _____

6. so fun much . We had

   _____

In the Group

Read each group of words. Then circle the word that does not belong.

Circle the shell with **blue** if the words are nouns.
Circle the shell with **green** if the words are adjectives.
Circle the shell with **yellow** if the words are verbs.

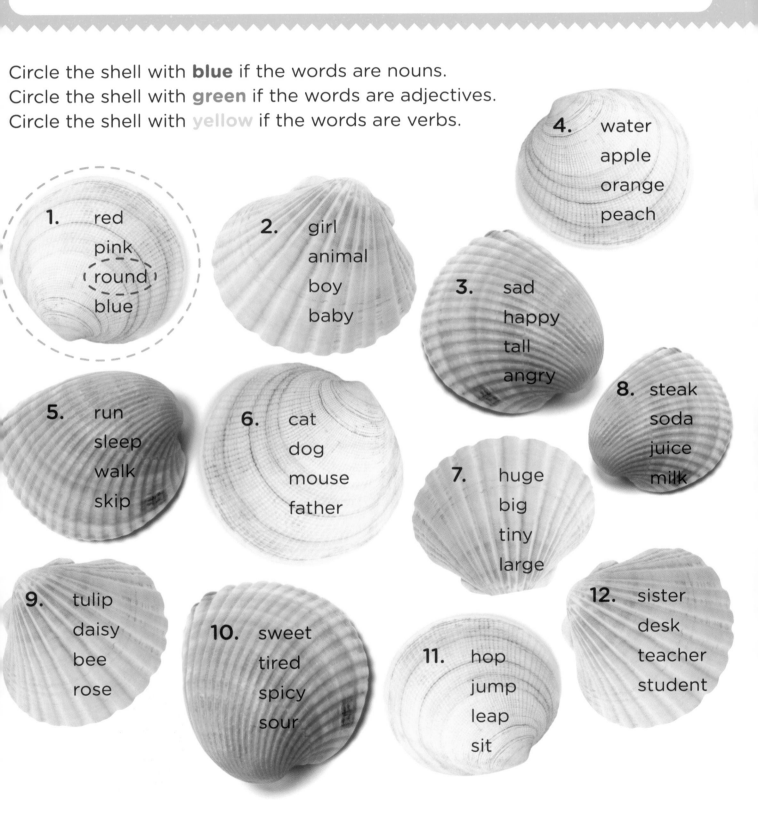

1. red
   pink
   round
   blue

2. girl
   animal
   boy
   baby

3. sad
   happy
   tall
   angry

4. water
   apple
   orange
   peach

5. run
   sleep
   walk
   skip

6. cat
   dog
   mouse
   father

7. huge
   big
   tiny
   large

8. steak
   soda
   juice
   milk

9. tulip
   daisy
   bee
   rose

10. sweet
    tired
    spicy
    sour

11. hop
    jump
    leap
    sit

12. sister
    desk
    teacher
    student

Hearing Syllables

Every word is made up of one or more syllables. Say these words aloud slowly. Clap on each syllable. Look at how the lines separate each word into syllables.

car $\boxed{1}$ rabbit (rab/bit) $\boxed{2}$ December (De/cem/ber) $\boxed{3}$

Read each word aloud slowly. Clap on the syllables. Then write the number of syllables in the box. Draw lines to show the syllables.

1. doc/tor $\boxed{2}$ 2. buck $\boxed{}$ 3. rooster $\boxed{}$

4. wheat $\boxed{}$ 5. November $\boxed{}$ 6. Saturday $\boxed{}$

7. person $\boxed{}$ 8. instead $\boxed{}$ 9. myself $\boxed{}$

10. understand $\boxed{}$ 11. public $\boxed{}$ 12. bulldozer $\boxed{}$

Find the words with two syllables in the word search. Words can go across or down. You should find six words.

P	A	T	R	O	S	U	P
U	W	E	O	A	P	C	E
B	R	D	O	C	T	O	R
L	E	A	S	B	A	I	S
I	N	S	T	E	A	D	O
C	U	M	E	I	V	J	N
R	P	E	R	D	I	Y	O
T	A	M	Y	S	E	L	F

Goody Bags

Divide up the treats equally. How many can you put in each bag? Use tally marks to keep track. Write the number per bag on the line to solve the problem.

$9 \div 3 = \underline{}$

$12 \div 2 = \underline{}$

$15 \div 3 = \underline{}$

Time to Write

Practice writing the letters in cursive.

Jj Jj

Kk Kk

Ll Ll

Mm Mm

$N\tilde{n}$ Nn

Oo Oo

Pp Pp

Qq Qq

$R\hat{r}$ Rr

Copy the number words in cursive.

one _____ two _____

three _____ four _____

136

Let's Get Healthy!

Complete the activity below.

These are all healthy foods:

breads and grains   **meats**
vegetables and fruits   **dairy foods** (milk and cheese)

Some foods are not good for you.

These foods are okay to eat sometimes:
fats (greasy foods)   **sweets** (candy)

Look at the foods below. Circle the food if it is a healthy food.
Draw an **X** over the food if it is not healthy.

Birthday

With an adult's help, fill out this birth certificate.
Tape a baby picture in the box, or draw a picture of yourself as a baby.

First Name: _____

Middle Name: _____

Last Name: _____

Who named me? _____

What does my name mean? _____

Date of birth: _____

Day of the week: _____

Time: _____

Weight: _____ Length: _____

My hair color: _____

My eye color: _____

When I was born, I looked the most like: _____

Hospital and hometown: _____

Tricky Tracks

Use regrouping to add or subtract. Then find the racetrack that has all the correct answers to the problems.

A

44
21
31
18
16
28
17
32

B

16
28
31
12
40
24
23
21

1.
$$\begin{array}{r} 14 \\ +\ 7 \\ \hline \end{array}$$

2.
$$\begin{array}{r} 22 \\ -\ 4 \\ \hline \end{array}$$

3.
$$\begin{array}{r} 23 \\ +\ 9 \\ \hline \end{array}$$

4.
$$\begin{array}{r} 25 \\ -\ 9 \\ \hline \end{array}$$

5.
$$\begin{array}{r} 38 \\ +\ 6 \\ \hline \end{array}$$

6.
$$\begin{array}{r} 33 \\ -\ 5 \\ \hline \end{array}$$

7.
$$\begin{array}{r} 25 \\ +\ 6 \\ \hline \end{array}$$

8.
$$\begin{array}{r} 24 \\ -\ 7 \\ \hline \end{array}$$

Family Tree

Complete the word family lists using words from inside the tree.
Then come up with one of your own words for each list.

ball

_____

_____

_____

gold

_____

_____

_____

tent

_____

_____

_____

munch

_____

_____

_____

tight

_____

_____

_____

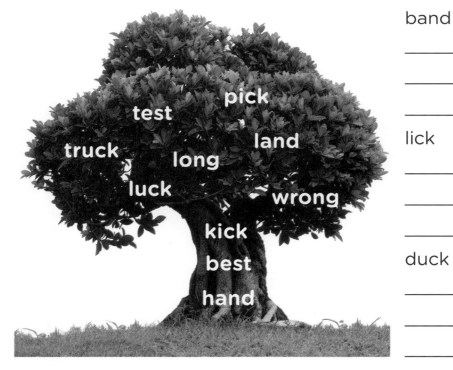

band

_____

_____

_____

lick

_____

_____

_____

duck

_____

_____

_____

west

_____

_____

_____

song

_____

_____

_____

Favorite Vacation

Many people take vacations in the summer. Complete the graph below by asking six people about their favorite vacation spot. Start at the bottom of the graph and color a square for each answer. Then answer the questions below.

Number of People	Beach	Mountains	Country	City
6				
5				
4				
3				
2				
1				

Vacation Places

1. Which place did people like best? _____

2. Which place did people like least? _____

3. Which place did people like second best? _____

4. What did you learn from making this graph? _____

_____

Packing Peanuts

There are 10 peanuts in each bag. Circle each group of 10 peanuts.
Count the extras, then write the numbers on the lines.

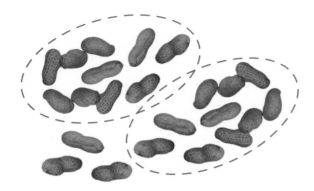

1. __2__ __3__ = __23__
   tens   ones

2. _____ _____ = _____
   tens   ones

3. _____ _____ = _____
   tens   ones

4. _____ _____ = _____
   tens   ones

5. _____ _____ = _____
   tens   ones

6. _____ _____ = _____
   tens   ones

Groups of Grapes

Count the number of groups and the number of grapes.
Solve the multiplication problems.

• 4 grapes in the group
• 1 group

4 x 1 = 4

1.

• 3 grapes
• 1 group

3 x 1 = _____

B

2.

• 5 grapes
• 1 group

5 x 1 = _____

T

3.

• 2 grapes
• 1 group

2 x 1 = _____

S

4.

• 2 grapes
• 2 groups

2 x 2 = _____

A

5.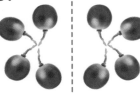

• 4 grapes
• 2 groups

4 x 2 = _____

L

6.

• 3 grapes
• 2 groups

3 x 2 = _____

E

Find each number above, and write the letter to complete the joke.

Where do the students sit during math class?

At the times ____ ____ B̶ ____ ____ ____
                5   4   3   8   6   2

The Car Wash

Read the story. Then complete the activity.

Emily's team wanted to go to soccer camp in the summer. The team members decided to have a car wash to raise money. They needed a way to spread the word. Emily helped put posters and flyers all around town. Everyone hoped the car wash would be a success.

On the day of the car wash, cars were lined up around the block! The girls split into two groups so they could wash the cars twice as fast. By the end of the day, the girls had raised enough money. The team would be able to go to soccer camp!

Connect each cause with its effect.

Cause

1. The team needed money for soccer camp.

2. They wanted to spread the word about the car wash.

3. Cars were lined up around the block.

4. The girls washed enough cars to raise the money.

Effect

a) The team would be able to go to soccer camp.

b) The team members decided to have a car wash.

c) The girls split into two groups to work faster.

d) Emily helped put posters and flyers around town.

Path to Poetry

Finish each poem below by writing a word from the box.
Choose a word that rhymes with the last word in the first line.

song	trees	care	feet

1. My little cat is soft and sweet,

   She plays with yarn with her tiny _____feet_____.

2. I love the summer days so long,

   I hear birds sing a happy _____.

3. Pumpkins, scarecrows, chilly breeze,

   Colored leaves fall from the _____.

4. Sandy beach and salty air,

   In the warm sun without a _____.

Now write your own poem! Think of summer days, friends, and things you
like to do. Below are some rhyming word pairs to help you.

fun/sun   **pool/cool**   **snug/bug**   **light/kite**   **sky/fly**   **day/play**

_____,

_____.

145

Dear Friend

Write a letter to a friend! Tell your friend about the things you are doing this summer. Then decorate it and give it to your friend to read.

_____
(date)

Dear _____

_____

_____

_____

_____

_____

_____

_____

_____

_____

_____

_____

_____ Your friend,

_____

Petal Pairs

Find each flower in the graph. First, count how many rows to the right.
Then count how many rows up. Write the number pair that shows the location.

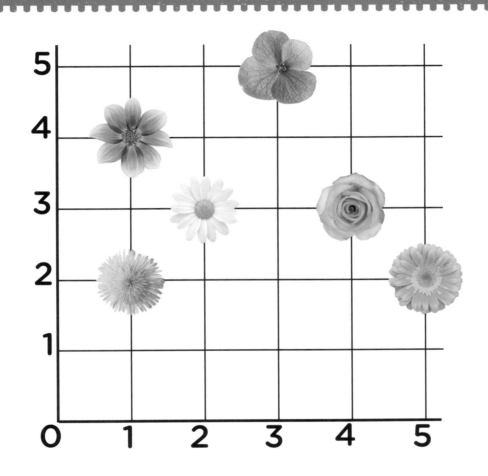

1.  _1_ , _2_

2.  _____ , _____

3.  _____ , _____

4.  _____ , _____

5.  _____ , _____

6.  _____ , _____

Beach Day

Antonyms are words that mean the opposite.
Connect each word with its antonym.

1. short   go   4. sad   out

2. stop   tall   5. high   low

3. light   dark   6. in   happy

Find two words in each sentence that are antonyms. Underline the words.

7. We jumped <u>over</u> the waves and swam <u>under</u> the water.

8. The cold water felt good on a hot day.

9. Our swimsuits were wet, but our towels were dry.

10. We found tiny shells and put them in a big bucket.

11. We went home when the day was turning into night.

12. As the sun slowly set, we quickly left the beach.

Sink or Float?

Some things will float on water, and some won't. What objects do you think will sink? What objects do you think will float? Find out by doing this experiment!

1. Gather the items shown below.

2. Fill a tub or bucket with water.

3. One at a time, place the objects in the water.

4. Circle the object below if it floats.

5. Cross out the object below if it sinks.

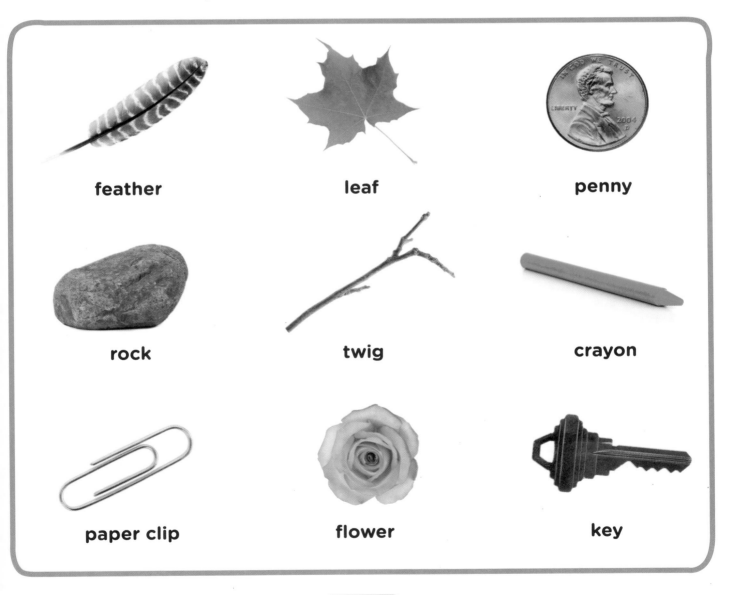

feather

leaf

penny

rock

twig

crayon

paper clip

flower

key

Shifting Shapes

Shapes can be put together to make new shapes.

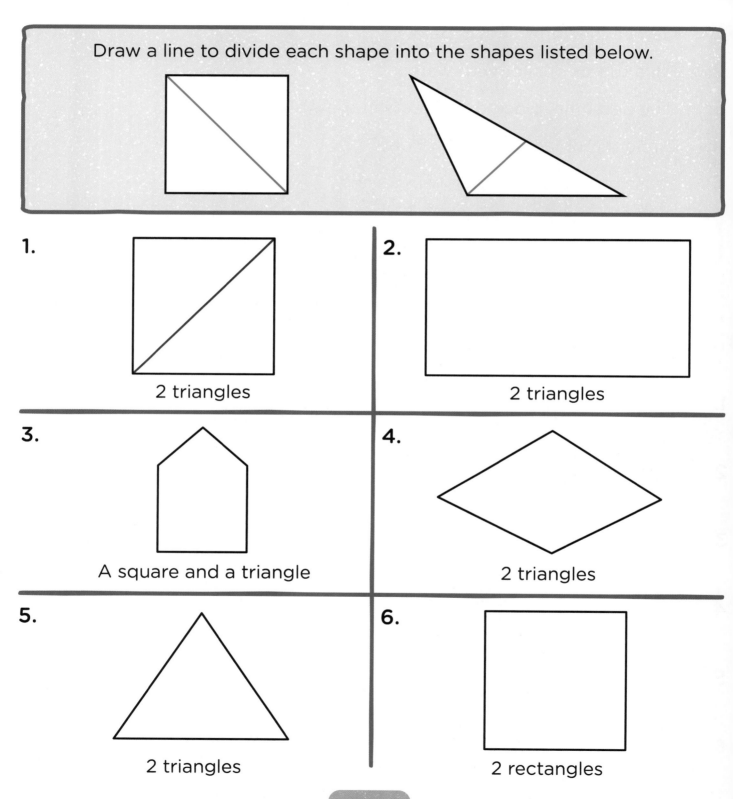

Draw a line to divide each shape into the shapes listed below.

1.

2 triangles

2.

2 triangles

3.

A square and a triangle

4.

2 triangles

5.

2 triangles

6.

2 rectangles

Speak Up!

Complete the activity below.

Quotation marks show the exact words that a speaker says. They go at the beginning and the end of the speaker's words, after the punctuation mark.

Connor said, "I love this movie."

"Me, too," Tony said.

Underline the words that the speaker says. Then put quotation marks around them.

1. Connor whispered to Tony, "Be quiet, please."

2. Tony replied, What did you say?

3. Conner asked, Can you eat your popcorn quietly?

4. Tony answered, I still can't hear you.

5. Your popcorn is too loud! Conner shouted.

6. Tony replied, Well, why didn't you speak up?

Three in a Row

Look at each picture and figure out whether it shows $\frac{1}{2}$, $\frac{1}{3}$, or $\frac{1}{4}$. Write the fraction in each box. Find three in a row with the same answer, and circle the row.

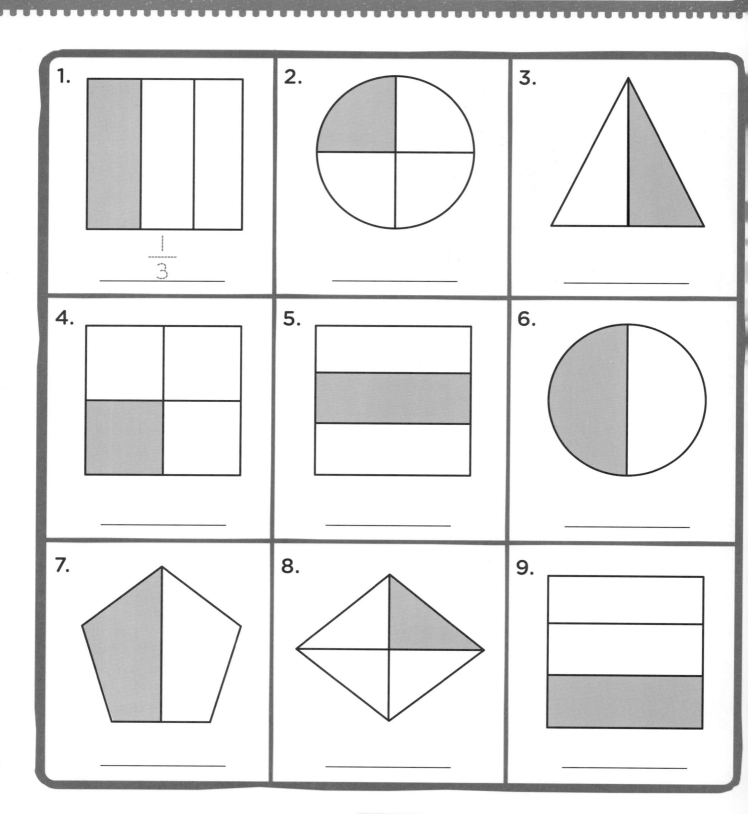

1.

$\frac{1}{3}$

2.

_____

3.

_____

4.

_____

5.

_____

6.

_____

7.

_____

8.

_____

9.

_____

Write Away

Practice writing the letters in cursive.

Ss Ss

Tt Tt

Uu Uu

Ww Ww

Xx Xx

Yy Yy

Zz Zz

Copy the days of the week in cursive.

Monday _____

Tuesday _____

Wednesday _____

Thursday _____

Friday _____

Saturday _____

Sunday _____

Run for the Money

Rounding numbers is easy! Here's how you do it.

When you use the $ sign, money less than
one dollar goes after the decimal point.

1¢ = $.01   5¢ = $.05   10¢ = $.10

Find the correct statements to make a path through the maze.

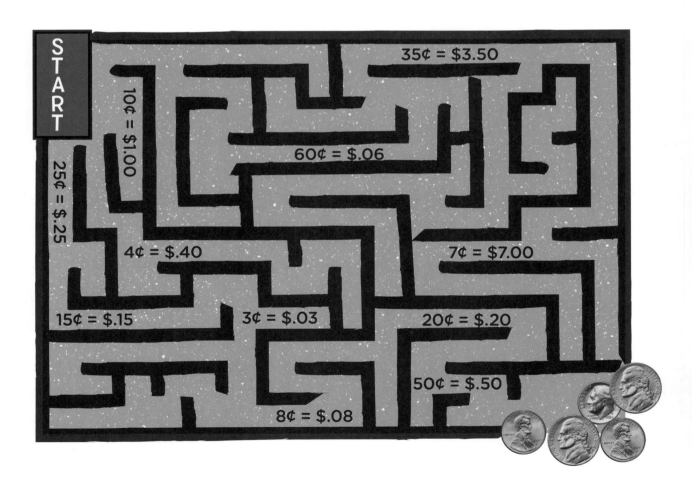

35¢ = $3.50

START

10¢ = $1.00

60¢ = $.06

25¢ = $.25

4¢ = $.40

7¢ = $7.00

15¢ = $.15   3¢ = $.03   20¢ = $.20

50¢ = $.50

8¢ = $.08

Answer Key

Page 4
3 4 5   8 9 10   18 19 20
11 12 13   6 7 8   14 15 16
12 13 14 15 16
21 22 23 24 25
8 7 6 5 4
20 19 18 17 16
AT THE COUNTER

Page 5
1. a
2. a
3. b
4. b

Page 6
2. 2 3 4 5 6 7 8 9 10 11 12
Pattern: +1
3. 3 6 9 12 15 18 21 24 27 30
Pattern: +3
4. 5 10 15 20 25 30 35 40 45
Pattern: +5

Page 7
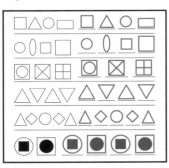

Page 8
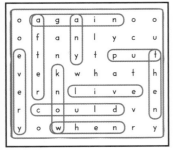

Page 9
Answers may include:
2 letters: or, to, he, me
3 letters: hoe, her, the, met, rot, hot, ore, toe, roe, hem
4 letters: more, home, tore, them, moth
5 letters: other
Big word: mother

Page 10
2. tiny, yellow
3. large, noisy
4. short, curly, soft
5. long, shady
6. crisp, sweet
7. new, tasty
8. fun, warm
9. smart, funny
10. spicy, hot

Page 11

1. $\begin{array}{r}4\\+3\\\hline7\end{array}$	$\begin{array}{r}5\\+1\\\hline6\end{array}$	2. $\begin{array}{r}2\\+6\\\hline8\end{array}$	$\begin{array}{r}4\\+0\\\hline4\end{array}$
3. $\begin{array}{r}1\\+7\\\hline8\end{array}$	$\begin{array}{r}3\\+3\\\hline6\end{array}$	4. $\begin{array}{r}0\\+5\\\hline5\end{array}$	$\begin{array}{r}2\\+2\\\hline4\end{array}$
5. $\begin{array}{r}4\\+1\\\hline5\end{array}$	$\begin{array}{r}2\\+8\\\hline10\end{array}$		$\begin{array}{r}1\\+6\\\hline7\end{array}$ $\begin{array}{r}8\\+1\\\hline9\end{array}$
7. $\begin{array}{r}5\\+4\\\hline9\end{array}$	$\begin{array}{r}5\\+5\\\hline10\end{array}$	8. $\begin{array}{r}0\\+9\\\hline9\end{array}$	$\begin{array}{r}3\\+7\\\hline10\end{array}$

Page 12
2. I left my lunch at home.
3. I can share my lunch.
4. Do you like apples?
5. Can I have a bite?
6. You are a good friend.

Page 13
2. sheep
3. shoe
4. shell
5. cheese
6. chicken
7. child
8. ship

Page 14

Page 15
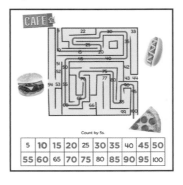

5	10	15	20	25	30	35	40	45	50
55	60	65	70	75	80	85	90	95	100

Page 16
1. This is my pet bird.
2.–3. Answers will vary.
4. What does the bird eat?
5.–6. Answers will vary.

Page 17
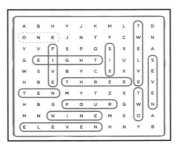

Page 18
2. 3
3. 2
4. 6
5. 8
6. 5
7. 1
8. 7
9. 9
10. 10
Rocket A

Page 19
2. cup
3. hat
4. dog
5. web
6. lid
7. zip
8. rug
9. van
10. Beginning
11. Ending
12. Beginning

Page 20
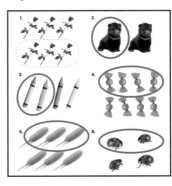

Page 21
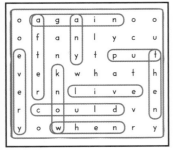

Page 22
51 52 53 54 55 56 57 58 59 60
61 62 63 64 65 66 67 68 69 70
71 72 73 74 75 76 77 78 79 80
81 82 83 84 85 86 87 88 89 90
91 92 93 94 95 96 97 98 99 100
TO ONE FUNDRED

Page 23
3
1
5
2
6
4
1. c
2. a
3. d
4. b

Page 24
1. There are 16 verbs: got, has, barks, chases, walk, play, is, loves, showed, jump, catch, go, is, named, comes, call
2.–6. Answers will vary.

Page 25
2. kitten
3. apple
4. baby
5. child
6. beach
7. milk
8. dinosaur
9. zoo
10. home

Page 26

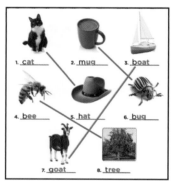

Page 27
1. socks
2. bike
3. trees
4. foxes
5. rocks
6. tire
7. wheel
8. ribbon

Page 28

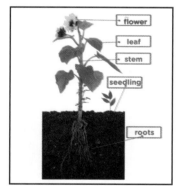

1. cat
2. mug
3. boat
4. bee
5. hat
6. bug
7. goat
8. tree

Page 29

flower
leaf
stem
seedling
roots

Page 30
1. 2 + 3 = 5
   3 + 2 = 5
2. 6 + 4 = 10
   4 + 6 = 10
3. 5 + 2 = 7
   2 + 5 = 7
4. 2 + 9 = 11
   9 + 2 = 11
5. 6 + 3 = 9
   3 + 6 = 9
6. 9 + 1 = 10
   1 + 9 = 10
7. 7 + 5 = 12
   5 + 7 = 12
8. 3 + 8 = 11
   8 + 3 = 11

Page 31
2. Our plane landed in Honolulu.
3. Then Amy and I flew to Maui.
4. Amy's sister Peg lives in Maui.
5. Peg took Amy and me swimming.
6. I want to go to Hawaii again!

Page 32

Page 33
2. 1 5 9 13 17 21 25
Pattern: +4
3. 14 12 10 8 6 4 2
Pattern: -2
4. 3 6 9 12 15 18 21
Pattern: +3
5. 10 9 8 7 6 5 4 3
Pattern: -1
6. 10 15 20 25 30 35 40
Pattern: +5

Page 34
Answers will vary.

Page 35
2. early
3. early
4. early
5. late
6. late

Page 36
2. pounds
3. ounces
4. ounces
5. pounds
6. pounds
7. pounds
8. ounces

Page 37
Runner A is the winner.
2. 2:30
3. 4:30
4. 6:00
5. 8:00
6. 5:30
7. 7:00
8. 11:00
9. 12:30

Page 38
2. tube
3. cane
4. tape
5. hid
6. hope
7. fine
8. bit
9. not
10. mope
11. mad
12. rode

Page 39
2. bell
3. wash
4. tax
5. jar
6. sky

Page 40
Today was a very windy day! On my way to school, my hat blew down the street. My hair was a mess! At school, I dropped my notebook and papers went everywhere. My best friend Joshua helped me catch them. When I got home, a branch had blown off our tree. It fell in the yard. When the lights went out, we had to use candles to see. It was fun to eat dinner with candles. Later, Dad told us a scary story. Then, when I was in bed, the wind shook the windows. It was spooky!

Page 41
1. 7
2. 9
3. 8
4. 10
5. 14
6. 11
7. 13
8. 12
9. 15
EIGHT!

Page 42
2. Larry
3. Garry
4. Both
5. Larry
6. Garry

Page 43
2. football
3. cupcake
4. starfish
5. sunshine
6. fireplace
7. doorbell
8. rainbow

Page 44
Ice is a solid.
Water is a liquid.
Steam is a gas.
2. solid
3. gas
4. solid
5. liquid
6. liquid
7. gas
8. solid
9. solid
10. liquid

Page 45

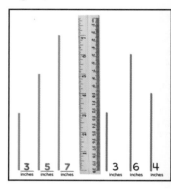

Page 46

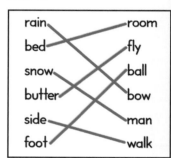

1. butterfly
2. football
3. bedroom
4. snowman
5. sidewalk
6. rainbow

Page 47

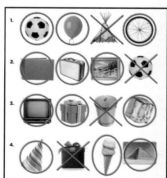

Page 48
1. 5 apples
2. 4 cookies
3. 11 toppings
4. 10 fries
5. 12 berries
6. 8 peanuts

Page 49

Answers will vary.
2. book
3. pen
4. paper

Page 50

2. bed, chair, dresser, table
3. breakfast, dinner, lunch, snack
4. book, desk, pencil, student
5. autumn, fall, summer, winter
6. beach, mall, park, zoo
7. crab, lobster, starfish, whale
8. goldfish, kitten, mouse, puppy

Page 51

2. It was a warm and breezy summer day.
3. My brother Carlos swam in the ocean.
4. I played in the sand and built a big sand castle.
5. Carlos and I hunted for shells along the seashore.
6. We found pink, white, and purple shells.
7. My dad made a big bonfire to cook dinner.
8. We ate hot dogs, chips, and crispy vegetables.
9. The ocean smelled fresh and salty.
10. Do you think we can come back next weekend?

Page 52

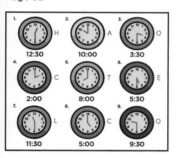

CHOCO-LATE

Page 53

2. Mr.
3. Dr.
4. Jr.
5. Sr.
6. Ms.
7. Jan.
8. Feb.
9. Tues.
10. Thurs.
11. Aug.
12. Sun.
13. Sat.
14. Sept.
15. Dec.
16. Mon.
17. Oct.
18. Wed.
19. Fri.
20. Nov.
21. Apr.
22. Mar.

Page 54

These objects should be circled:
Winter: mittens, coat, boots, sweater, wool hat
Spring: T-shirt, dress, tank top, sandals, raincoat, shorts, skirt
Summer: tank top, shorts, sunglasses, sandals, T-shirt, dress
Fall: coat, jeans, gloves, sweater, scarf

Page 55

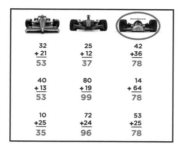

Page 56

2. bee
3. rain
4. pie
5. bike
6. toe
7. tube
8. cry
9. glue
10. boat
11. hay
12. bow
13. cake
14. leaf
Long a: rain, hay, cake
Long e: bee, leaf
Long i: pie, bike, cry
Long o: rose, toe, boat, bow
Long u: tube, glue

Page 57

1 2 3 4 5 6 7 8 9 10
11 12 13 14 15 16 17 18 19 20
21 22 23 24 25 26 27 28 29 30
31 32 33 34 35 36 37 38 39 40
41 42 43 44 45 46 47 48 49 50
51 52 53 54 55 56 57 58 59 60
61 62 63 64 65 66 67 68 69 70
71 72 73 74 75 76 77 78 79 80
81 82 83 84 85 86 87 88 89 90
91 92 93 94 95 96 97 98 99 100

Page 58

2   4   6   8   10
12 14 16 18 20
22 24 26 28 30

10 20 30 40 50
60 70 80 90 100
IN THE FOUR-EST

Page 59

1. b
2. snakes, mosquitoes, alligators
3. Answers will vary. It is hot, steamy, and damp.
4. Answers will vary.

Page 60

2. 2 quarters, 4 dimes, 2 nickels
3. 3 quarters, 3 nickels, 1 dime
4. 3 quarters, 2 dimes, 1 nickel
5. 3 quarters, 2 dimes, 5 pennies

Page 61

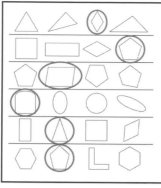

Page 62

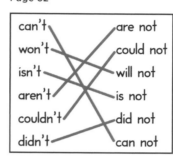

2. couldn't
3. can't
4. aren't
5. isn't
6. won't

Page 63

Would you like to come with me to the store? I am going to buy new school clothes. I would like to buy new shoes and a coat. After we shop, we can go out to lunch. Do you want burgers or pizza?

Mia and her friends were so excited! They were going to the zoo. At the zoo, they saw all kinds of wild animals. Which do you think was Mia's favorite? Of all the animals, Mia liked the giraffes the best.

Daniel was nervous. Today was the first game of the baseball playoffs. How many games had the Tigers won this season? Daniel was proud they had won all games but one. Oh no! It was starting to rain. They would have to wait until tomorrow to play.

Page 64

2. D
3. D
4. E
5. E
6. D
7. D
8. I
9. E
10. I

Page 65

1. 3 < 30
   21 = 21
   44 > 14
2. 10 > 3 + 1
   6 < 5 + 4
   8 = 3 + 5
3. 2 + 1 < 2 + 2
   3 + 4 > 6 + 0
   2 + 8 = 8 + 2
4. 7 + 1 < 4 + 5
   5 + 1 = 3 + 3
   4 + 2 > 3 + 1
5. 5 - 3 < 6 - 2
   8 - 3 > 7 - 5
   6 - 3 = 10 - 7
6. 8 - 7 = 5 - 4
   4 - 0 > 7 - 4
   8 - 8 < 7 - 2
7. 1 + 4 = 10 - 5
   6 + 2 > 6 - 3
   2 + 0 < 10 - 7
8. 10 - 4 < 4 + 4
   9 - 5 = 2 + 2
   6 - 1 > 3 + 0

Page 66

Answers will vary.
1. closes
2. shout
3. eats
4. opens

Page 67

1. 3, 1, 2, 4
2. 3, 4, 2, 1
3. 1, 3, 4, 2
4. 3, 1, 2, 4

Page 68

Across
2. 6
3. 1
4. 8
6. 10
8. 5

Down
1. 2
2. 7
5. 3
7. 9
8. 4

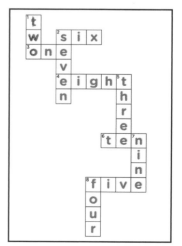

Page 69
Answers will vary.

Page 70
2. bald eagle
3. Liberty Bell
4. flag
5. "The Star-Spangled Banner"
6. Capitol

Page 71
2. 40¢
3. $1.10
4. 75¢
5. $1.15

Page 72
2. 22
3. 52
4. 32
5. 42
6. 81
7. 11
8. 70
9. 61
Bottom bunny

Page 73
Answers will vary but could include:
2. pen, hen, ten; short e
3. sit, bit, kit; short i
4. mop, cop, top; short o
5. mug, hug, rug; short u
6. bake, cake, lake; long a
7. heat, neat, beat; long e
8. dine, nine, vine; long i
9. rope, hope, cope; long o
10. true, blue, glue; long u
11. snack
12. moon
13. head
14. broom

Page 74
2. 2 + 3 + 4 = 9
3. 5 + 5 + 7 = 17
4. 3 + 6 + 1 = 10
5. 8 + 2 + 3 = 13
6. 2 + 2 + 4 = 8
7. 1 + 5 + 6 = 12
8. 9 + 8 + 3 = 20
9. 7 + 6 + 1 = 14
10. 3 + 3 + 5 = 11
11. 8 + 7 + 3 = 18
12. 2 + 4 + 1 = 7

Page 75

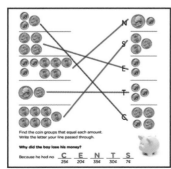

Page 76
1. 200 million
2. b) $\frac{2}{3}$ cup dish detergent and c) 1 gallon water
3. can, hanger, hula hoop
4. 2, 1, 4, 3

Page 77
2. i
3. n
4. o
5. s
6. a
7. u
8. r
DINOSAUR

Page 78
2. ball, blank, book, brook
3. cave, clown, cold, creek
4. day, desk, dinner, drain
5. pail, people, plane, proud
6. raccoon, rhino, roam, rust
7. sale, slide, snake, story
8. team, tide, tool, trail

Page 79
1. 4 + 2 = 6
   2 + 4 = 6
   6 − 2 = 4
   6 − 4 = 2
2. 7 + 3 = 10
   3 + 7 = 10
   10 − 7 = 3
   10 − 3 = 7
3. 4 + 8 = 12
   8 + 4 = 12
   12 − 4 = 8
   12 − 8 = 4
4. 3 + 4 = 7
   4 + 3 = 7
   7 − 4 = 3
   7 − 3 = 4
5. 10 + 5 = 15
   5 + 10 = 15
   15 − 5 = 10
   15 − 10 = 5
6. 6 + 5 = 11
   5 + 6 = 11
   11 − 6 = 5
   11 − 5 = 6

Page 80

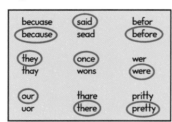

1. were
2. our
3. said
4. because

Page 81
1. last summer
2. the mountains
3. yellow flowers
4. a doe and her fawn
5. croaking, chirping

Page 82
Mammals: deer, monkey, skunk, lion
Reptiles: lizard, rattlesnake, alligator, dinosaur
Fish: catfish, tuna, trout, eel
Birds: chicken, robin, eagle, parrot

Page 83
1. 3 + 4 = 7
   8 − 4 = 4
2. 10 − 1 = 11
   10 − 5 = 5
3. 8 − 3 = 5
   9 + 4 = 13
4. 6 + 7 = 13
   16 − 8 = 8
5. 5 + 9 = 14
   9 − 7 = 2
6. 9 + 8 = 17
   5 − 4 = 1
7. 12 − 7 = 5
   8 + 7 = 15
8. 13 − 3 = 10
   3 + 7 = 10

Page 84

Answers will vary.
2. big
3. floppy
4. long

Page 85
Across
1. thank you
4. open
7. please
9. may

Down
2. nice
3. sorry
5. excuse
6. smile
8. love
10. shake

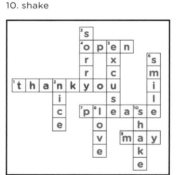

Page 86

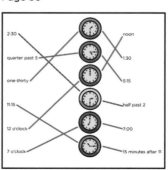

Page 87
Answers will vary.

Page 88
2. 75¢
3. $1.50
4. $12
5. $15,000
6. $35
7. $5
8. $1

Page 89
2. sugar
3. 5
4. 4
5. peanut butter

Page 90
1. 33
2. 23
3. 30
4. 11
5. 20
6. 32
7 51
8. 31
9. 22
10. 21
The blue van wins.

Page 91
1. stop
2. skunk
3. snake
4. spoon
5. sleep
6. star
7. smoke
8. slide
9. spill
10. snail
11. smell
12. skate
sk: skunk, skate
sl: sleep, slide
sn: snake, snail
sm: smoke, smell
sp: spoon, spill
st: stop, star

Page 92
2. o
3. o
4. t
5. s
6. t
7. e
8. p
9. s
FOOTSTEPS

Page 93
1. 11
2. 47
3. 20
4. 30
5. 87
6. 34
7. 21
8. 79
9. 89
10. 13
11. 98
TEN-NIS SHOES

Page 94
1. the moon
2. five
3. Chapter 3
4. Chapter 1
5. Chapter 4

Page 95
2. ship
3. bicycle
4. airplane
5. helicopter
6. hot air balloon
7. motorcycle
8. sailboat
9. scooter
10. train
11. truck
12. skateboard

Page 96
2. Yes
3. No
4. Yes
5. Yes
6. No

Page 97

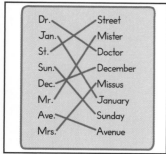

2. Tues., Nov. 10
3. Fri., Oct. 2
4. Sat., Aug. 8

Page 98
2. pink
3. purple
4. orange
5. gray
6. Answers will vary.

Page 99
2. My coach is Mrs. Jones.
3. Every Thursday we have a soccer game.
4. Our soccer team plays in April and May.
5. In June there is a big game to end the season.
6. Even Mr. Jones comes to cheer on the team.

Page 100

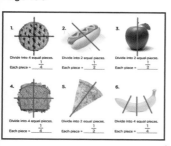

Page 101

1. Jill has five tulips, and Jon has six roses. How many flowers do they have altogether? **11** flowers
2. Ethan kicked five goals at the game, and so did Bruce. How many goals did they kick together? **10** goals
3. Betty had twelve carrots. She gave six to Fran. How many carrots does Betty have left? **6** carrots
4. Tom has two ladybugs, three beetles, and one cricket in his bug collection. How many bugs are there altogether? **6** bugs
5. Brian had fifteen pieces of candy. He gave five to his brother. How many does he have left? **10** pieces
6. The giant ice cream cone has two scoops of vanilla, two scoops of chocolate, and one scoop of strawberry. How many scoops does it have in total? **5** scoops
7. Lynn had sixteen stickers in her collection. She gave eight to Nora. How many stickers does Lynn have left? **8** stickers
8. Drew scored seven points during the game. Then he scored three more during overtime. How many points in total did he score? **10** points
9. Dave has ten fingers and ten toes. How many fingers and toes does he have altogether? **20** fingers and toes

Page 102
Answers will vary.

Page 103
2. thermometer
3. ruler
4. ruler
5. scale
6. measuring cup
7. ruler
8. scale

Page 104
1. 1, 5, 2, 3, 4; spaghetti
2. 5, 4, 3, 1, 2; brushed my teeth
3. 4, 2, 5, 1, 3; toast with jam

Page 105
2. 34
3. 45
4. 54
5. 27
6. 37
7. 48
8. 73
9. 86
10. 68
Runner A wins.

Page 106
1. broom
2. glue
3. cloud
4. cry
5. frog
6. grass
7. block
8. prince
9. flag
10. draw
11. plane
12. train

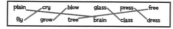

Page 107

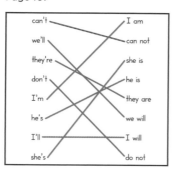

Page 108
2. marsupials
3. pouches
4. joey
5. up to 10 months

Page 109
2. 21
3. 32
4. 23
5. 30
6. 44
7. 42
8. 50
I ADDMIRE YOU!

Page 110
1. True
2. False
3. True
4. False
5. True

Page 111
2, 4, 3, 1

Page 112
2. teacher
3. mail carrier
4. veterinarian
5. doctor
6. clerk
7. bus driver
8. dentist
9. nurse
10. police officer

Page 113
1. favorite meals
2.–4. Answers will vary.

Page 114
1. ponies
2. babies
3. berries
4. daddies
5. b
6. c
7. a
8. b

Page 115
2. afternoon
3. morning
4. morning
5. night
6. afternoon
7. night
8. night

Page 116
2. 3:15
3. 5:45
4. 10:45
5. 7:15
6. 11:45

Page 117
2. The bat belongs to Pam. Pam's bat
3. The baseball belongs to Pam. Pam's baseball
4. The music belongs to Sam. Sam's music.

5. Sam plays the piano. He likes music. Sam
6. Pam plays baseball. She likes sports. Pam
7. Sam and Pam are friends. They like to play. Sam and Pam
8. Sam is cold. He is wearing a sweater. Sam

Page 118
2. yes
3. no
4. no
5. yes
6. no

Page 119
5 10 15 20 25 30
1 3 5 7 9 11
3 6 9 12 15 18
4 8 12 16 20 24

Page 120
The page is completed when letters and name are written in cursive.

Page 121
2. koala
3. giraffe
4. rhino
5. tiger
6. zebra
7. snake
8. elephant
9. penguin
10. lion
11. monkey
12. hippo
Bonus word: alligator

Page 122
Answers will vary.

Page 123
1. ship
2. wheel
3. thumb
4. three
5. whistle
6. shoe
7. chair
8. thin
9. cheese
10. cheek
11. shell
12. whale
ch: chair, cheese, cheek
sh: ship, shoe, shell
th: thumb, three, thin
wh: wheel, whistle, whale

Page 124
2. vet
3. water
4. walks
5. food
6. play
7. love

P	L	A	Y	U	W	A	R
F	O	N	W	F	A	R	
A	V	L	P	O	L	W	
V	E	T	B	O	K	U	
R	E	M	A	D	S	E	
E	W	A	T	E	R	T	
S	O	T	H	A	C	H	

Page 125
Answers will vary.

Page 126
2. 18
3. 23
4. 29
5. 37
6. 16
7. 38
8. 26
BIG HANDS!

Page 127
1. b
2. a
3. An owner needs to give a dog food, water, exercise, and take it to a vet for checkups and shots.
4. Answers will vary.

Page 128
Row 1: MONKEY
Row 2: TURKEY
Row 3: DONKEY

Page 129
2. 3 hours
3. 1 hour

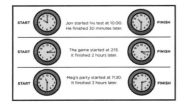

Page 130
1. little, small
2. run, jog
3. fast, speedy
4. laugh, giggle
5. angry, mad
6. happy, glad
8. cooked
9. tasty
10. cold
11. chatted

Page 131
2. 29 30 31
3. 54 55 56
4. 16 17 18 19
5. 48 49 50 51
6. 32 33 34 35
7. 96 97 98 99 100
8. 61 62 63 64 65
10. 90 91 89
11. 20 19 18
12. 72 71 70 69
13. 80 79 78 77
14. 57 56 55 54
13. 29 28 27 26 25
14. 57 56 55 54
15. 29 28 27 26 25
16. 44 43 42 41 40

Page 132
1. I camped at the lake.
2. We put up a tent.
3. I slept in a sleeping bag.
4. We cooked over a fire.
5. I went fishing in the lake.
6. We had so much fun.

Page 133

Page 134
2. buck, 1
3. roost / er, 2
4. wheat, 1
5. No / vem / ber, 3
6. Sat / ur / day, 3
7. per / son, 2
8. in / stead, 2
9. my / self, 2
10. un / der / stand, 3
11. pub / lic, 2
12. bull / doz / er, 3

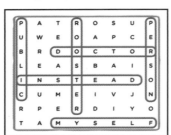

Page 135

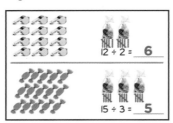

Page 136
The page is completed when letters and words are written in cursive.

Page 137
These objects should be circled: grapes, bread, steak, turkey, lettuce, yogurt, cheese, carrots, cereal.
These objects should be crossed out: candy bar, cake, french fries.

Page 138
Answers will vary.

Page 139
1. 21
2. 18
3. 32
4. 16
5. 44
6. 28
7. 31
8. 17
Track A

Page 140
ball: wall, call, answers vary
munch: lunch, punch, answers vary
gold: cold, told, answers vary
tight: night, light, answers vary
tent: went, sent, answers vary
band: hand, land, answers vary
west: best, test, answers vary
lick: kick, pick, answers vary
song: long, wrong, answers vary
duck: truck, luck, answers vary

Page 141
Answers will vary.

Page 142
2. 1 ten, 5 ones = 15
3. 2 tens, 0 ones = 20
4. 1 ten, 9 ones = 19
5. 2 tens, 6 ones = 26
6. 3 tens, 1 one = 31

Page 143
1. 3 x 1 = 3
2. 5 x 1 = 5
3. 2 x 1 = 2
4. 2 x 2 = 4
5. 4 x 2 = 8
6. 3 x 2 = 6
At the times tables

Page 144
1. b
2. d
3. c
4. a

Page 145
2. song
3. trees
4. care
The poem at the bottom should have a rhyming word pair.

Page 146
The written letter will vary.

Page 147
2. 4, 3
3. 2, 3
4. 5, 2
5. 3, 5
6. 1, 4

Page 148
1. short, tall
2. stop, go
3. light, dark
4. sad, happy
5. high, low
6. in, out
8. cold, hot
9. wet, dry
10. tiny, big
11. day, night
12. slowly, quickly

Page 149
These objects should be circled: feather, leaf, twig, crayon, flower
These objects should be crossed out: penny, rock, paper clip, key

Page 150
Dividing lines can vary but may include the following:

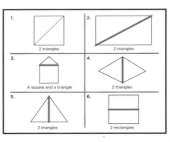

Page 151
2. Tony replied, "What did you say?"
3. Conner asked, "Can you eat your popcorn quietly?"
4. Tony answered, "I still can't hear you."
5. "Your popcorn is too loud!" Conner shouted.
6. Tony replied, "Well, why didn't you speak up?"

Page 152

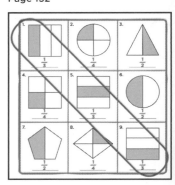

Page 153
The page is completed when the words are written in cursive.

Page 154

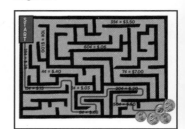

FlashK⚡ds

Punch out flash cards!

Say the name of each picture. Which of the following begin with the **ch** sound?

1

A **verb** is an action word. Which of the following words are verbs?

run

everywhere

skip

same

sleep

also

friend

jump

3

Tell whether each is a **solid**, a **liquid**, or a **gas**.

1. book   2. water

3. air   4. juice

5. ice   6. pencil

5

An **adjective** is a word that describes something. Find the adjective in each sentence.

1. Tommy is a smart boy.

2. Jenny lost her red pencil.

3. Gabby has a new cell phone.

7

What is the contraction for each?

1. can not

2. did not

3. is not

4. could not

9

Match the synonyms.

work

nag

smart

start

bother

begin

wise

job

11

FlashKids

Punch out flash cards!

Estimate the price for each item.

1. $2.39

   $239

2. $5.89

   59¢

3. $19.98

   $1.98

Figure out the pattern in each row of numbers. Fill in the missing number.

a. 3, 6, 9, _____, 15, 18

b. 24, 20, 16, 12, _____, 4

c. _____, 14, 21, 28, 35, 42

d. 15, 20, 25, _____, 35, 40

e. 100, 90, _____, 70, 60, 50

Answer **more** or **less** for each number sentence.

a. 4 + 5 is _____ than 10.

b. 8 + 8 is _____ than 12.

c. 7 + 6 is _____ than 17.

d. 11 + 3 is _____ than 9.

6

4

2

Figure out the sign (+, −) that is missing for each number sentence.

a. 4 ☐ 5 = 9

b. 13 ☐ 8 = 5

c. 6 ☐ 0 = 6

d. 19 ☐ 3 = 22

Which pictures can be divided into two equal halves?

Add or subtract.

a.   33
  − 7

b.   24
  + 21

c.   63
  − 26

d.   81
  + 13

e.   19
  + 12

f.   76
  − 34

12

10

8

FlashKids

Punch out flash cards!

Identify the cause and the effect in each sentence.

1. Eddy wanted a new bike so he helped with chores around the house.

2. Mary needed a good grade on her math test so she studied every day.

13

Which words are spelled incorrectly?

friend   pritty

weird

becuz

candle

bisiness

funy   **school**

15

What does each abbreviation stand for?

Mr.   Dr.

Ms.

Nov.

St.

Wed.

Ave.

17

Think of 3 words that rhyme with each word.

1. clue

2. grade

3. treat

19

Think of three adjectives to describe the bear.

21

Unscramble the underlined words.

1. An elephant is a big <u>lamina</u>.

2. He is the teacher. I am the <u>dtnesut</u>.

3. I am tired. I'm going to <u>eples</u>.

4. A camera takes a <u>curtpei</u>.

23

Delilah didn't hear her alarm today. School starts at 8:00. What time does her clock say? Will she get there in time?

Regroup to add.

a. 17
   + 8

b. 37
   + 6

c. 24
   + 9

d. 42
   + 8

Add.

a. 4 tens + 2 ones=

b. 6 tens + 7 ones=

c. 7 tens + 9 ones=

d. 2 tens + 3 ones=

18

16

14

Corey bought 24 donuts to take to school: 6 chocolate, 8 powdered, and 10 frosted. He ate one and a half of the frosted on his way to school. He dropped 1 powdered in front of the classroom. There are 21 students in his class. Will he get to eat another full donut?

Maya has $20. She wants to buy a pair of sandals for $8.97 and sunglasses for $7.59. She needs to have enough money left over to take the bus home for $2. Can she buy her items?

Compare the equations. Choose <, >, or =.

a. 15 ☐ 8 + 7

b. 37 ☐ 44

c. 6 + 6 ☐ 8 – 3

d. 21 ☐ 56

e. 17 + 3 ☐ 30 – 10

f. 44 – 19 ☐ 23

24

22

20

FlashKids

Punch out flash cards!

Find and correct the misspelled words.

Tommy went to the zu. He saw an elefant, a jiraf, and a hipopawtimus. He ait a burger and fries for lunch. Then he saw a giant lyon sleeping in a caig.

25

Which word in each group doesn't belong?

1. coat, mittens, sandals, boots, scarf

2. pig, bear, camel, boat, dog

3. book, brush, crayons, pencil, ruler

27

An **adjective** is a word that describes a **noun**. Find the adjectives in each sentence.

1. Brittany likes to comb her long brown hair.

2. Jon rode his blue bike to the sunny beach.

3. Tim's dog is big and strong.

29

Say the name of each picture aloud. Then think of a word that rhymes with the name.

1.

2.

3.

31

Which word in each group is a **noun**?

1.   tall   happy
     red   house

2.   cup   hot
     hairy   noisy

3.   bright   hard
     desk   wet

4.   loud   water
     round   long

33

Rewrite each sentence with the correct capitalization and punctuation.

1. Claire and johnny Don't like roller coasters

2. does Regina have Running Shoes

3. My favorite foods are potatoes Burgers and pickles Yum

35

FlashKids

Punch out flash cards!

What is the number value for each?

a. 4 tens and 3 ones

b. 1 ten and 8 ones

c. 5 tens and 2 ones

d. 6 tens and 7 ones

Find the subtraction problems in the puzzle. Problems can go across or down.

17	7	6	4	2
2	2	15	4	9
15	8	6	0	11
8	3	0	7	3
3	5	6	8	8

Match each clock to the time.

1.  half past 2

2.  15 minutes after 11

3.  quarter past 5

30

28

26

Count backwards from 50.

50 _____ 48 47 46 _____ 44

43 42 41 40 39 _____ _____

36 35 34 _____ 32 31 30 29

28 27 _____ 25 24 23 _____

21 20 19 18 17 16 15 _____

13 12 11 _____ 9 8 7 6 5

_____ 3 2 1

Would you use ounces or pounds to measure each object?

1. dog

2. television

3. flower

4. seashell

5. chair

Which groups can be divided in half?

36

34

32

Match the words to make compound words.

rain	book
note	day
ice	coat
birth	cube

Put the following words in alphabetical order.

parade
holiday
push
cheek
length
rush
useful
surprise
imagine
whom

What is each animal? Is it a **mammal**, a **reptile**, a **fish**, or a **bird**?

rooster

bear

sardine

lizard

shark

elephant

pigeon

crocodile

37

39

41

Tell whether each vehicle travels on **land**, **water**, or **air**.

1.    2.

3.    4.

Dear Caregiver,

The summer months provide plenty of time to prepare your learner for the new school year. During this time, it is important not only to review the skills your student is familiar with, but also to introduce new skills your student will be learning in the coming grade. Encourage your learner to work on the cards independently or review them together so you can provide help and encouragement when needed. The cards can be used as:

- An extra practice lesson
- A take-along activity
- Daily reinforcement
- Comprehensive review

This deck contains 44 questions reviewing math and language arts skills. An answer key is provided on cards 46–48.

Enjoy!

Card 17
Mr. = Mister
Ms. = Miss
Nov. = November
St. = Street
Weds. = Wednesday
Ave. = Avenue
Dr. = Doctor

Card 18
9:00, No

Card 19
Possible answers:
1. blue, new, do, flew, shoe
2. aid, braid, maid, paid, stayed
3. feet, meat, eat, sheet, heat

Card 20
A. =   B. <   C. >
D. <   E. =   F. >

Card 21
Possible answers: brown, tall, angry

Card 22
Yes

Card 23
1. animal   2. student
3. sleep   4. picture

Card 24
No

Card 25
zoo, elephant, giraffe, hippopotamus, ate, lion, cage

Card 26
1. quarter past 5
2. half past 2
3. 15 minutes after 11

Card 27
1. sandals   2. boat
3. brush

Card 28
17-2 = 15   8-3 = 5
6-4 = 2   4-4 = 0
11-9 = 2

Card 29
1. long, brown
2. blue, sunny
3. big, strong

Card 30
A. 43   B. 18
C. 52   D. 67

Card 31
Possible answers:
1. coat, float, vote, wrote
2. tree, see, me, we
3. rat, bat, sat, mat

43

45

47

Write the fraction for each problem.

a. 1 of a whole divided into 4 equal pieces

b. 1 of a whole divided into 2 equal pieces

c. 1 of a whole divided into 3 equal pieces

42

Tell whether you would use a measuring cup, a scale, a ruler, or a thermometer to measure each.

1. temperature of the ocean water

2. width of a book

3. amount of oatmeal for a cookie recipe

4. weight of a bag of apples

40

Count the coins in each group that equal 70¢.

1.

_____

2.

_____

38

Card 32
bread, apples

Card 33
1. house   2. cup
3. desk   4. water

Card 34
1. pounds   2. pounds
3. ounces   4. ounces
5. pounds

Card 35
1. Claire and Johnny don't like roller coasters.
2. Does Regina have running shoes?
3. My favorite foods are potatoes, burgers, and pickles. Yum!

Card 36
49, 45, 38, 37, 33, 26, 22, 14, 10, 4

Card 37
raincoat   notebook
icecube   birthday

Card 38
1. 2 quarters, 4 nickels
2. 2 quarters, 2 dimes

Card 39
cheek, holiday, imagine, length, parade, push, rush, surprise, useful, whom

Card 40
1. thermometer
2. ruler
3. measuring cup
4. a scale

Card 41
mammals: bear, elephant
reptiles: lizard, crocodile
fish: sardine, shark
birds: rooster, pigeon

Card 42
A. 1/4   B. 1/2   C. 1/3

Card 43
1. water   2. air
3. land   4. land

Card 44
Ants are fast!

Card 1
cheese, chicken

Card 2
A. less   B. more
C. less   D. more

Card 3
run, jump, skip, sleep

Card 4
A. +3: 12   B. -4: 8   C. +7: 7
D. +5: 30   E. -10: 80

Card 5
1. solid   2. liquid   3. gas
4. liquid 5. solid   6. solid

Card 6
1. $2.39   2. 59¢   3. $19.98

Card 7
1. smart   2. red   3. new

Card 8
A. 26   B. 45   C. 37   D. 94
E. 31   F. 42

Card 9
1. can't   2. didn't
3. isn't   4. couldn't

Card 10
stop sign, star, cake

Card 11
work/job   nag/bother
smart/wise begin/start

Card 12
A. +   B. –
C. – , +   D. +

Card 13
1. cause: Eddy wanted a new bike
effect: he helped with chores
2. cause: Mary needed a good grade
effect: she studied every day

Card 14
A. 42   B. 67
C. 79   D. 23

Card 15
pretty, because, business, funny

Card 16
A. 25   B. 43
C. 33   D. 50

Solve the puzzle when:

t=2   r=7   s=6   n=3
e=8   f=0   a=9

___   ___   ___   ___
10 – 1   2 + 1   8 – 6   12 – 6

___   ___   ___
12 – 3   5 + 2   4 + 4

___   ___   ___   ___ !
7 – 7   6 + 3   3 + 3   4 – 2

48   **46**   **44**

FlashKids

SUMMER

2nd Grade

Track your progress throughout the summer!

Add a sticker after completing each set of activity pages. Do one set a week!

When all 10 weeks are finished you have earned your certificate!

Progress Chart

Summer Week	Activities	Date Completed	Award Sticker
1	Pages 4–18		
2	Pages 19–34		
3	Pages 35–50		
4	Pages 51–66		
5	Pages 67–82		
6	Pages 83–98		
7	Pages 99–114		
8	Pages 115–130		
9	Pages 131–146		
10	Pages 147–155		

FlashKids
SUMMER
2nd Grade

CONGRATULATIONS!

Presented to:

_____

for successfully completing all ten sections of the

FLASH KIDS 2ND GRADE SUMMER WORKBOOK